JOHN CARPENTER'S
NIGHT TERRORS

Series created by
JOHN CARPENTER and SANDY KING

STORM KING
COMICS

GRAVEYARD MOON

Written by STEVE NILES
Pencils by STEPHEN B. SCOTT
Inks by RODNEY RAMOS
Colors by LOVERN KINDZIERSKI
Lettering by JANICE CHIANG
Edited by SANDY KING
Cover art by KELLEY JONES and MICHELLE MADSEN
Book Design by SEAN SOBCZAK
Title Treatment by JOHN GALATI

Publishers: John Carpenter & Sandy King
Managing Editor: Sean Sobczak
Storm King Office Coordinator: Antwan Johnson
Publicity by Sphinx PR - Elysabeth Galati

John Carpenter's Night Terrors: GRAVEYARD MOON, September 2020.
Published by Storm King Comics, a division of Storm King Productions, Inc.

MATURE READERS

STORMKINGCOMICS.COM

 STORMKINGCOMICS   @STORMKINGCOMICS   STORMKINGCOMICS   JOHNCARPENTE

aveyard Moon.

d finding a good home for some horror.

member when Sandy King was talking about getting into comics. It was an idea she had,
v to bring good horror comics to print, working with independent creators. I was all for it.
od creator-owned comic publishers are hard to come by when you work for yourself, and if
eone is going to be all horror, then I am IN.

talked to other publishers and writers and artists to learn more about how it was done. But
tly, she talked about what we creators needed in a publisher. Then being the innovator that
is, she went and started Storm King Comics. Built entirely from the ground up by Sandy
j and John Carpenter, Storm King is one the most supportive comic publishers I know. They
ously care about writers and artists and allow us the freedom to just create the stories we
e up with. And the catalogue they've put out is solid, from original series like **Asylum** and
Standoff to anthologies like **Tales for a HalloweeNight**.

ing horror with Storm King is an honor.

ch brings me to **Graveyard Moon**.

rted the story with the memory of a funeral. At the same time, I had been watching a ton of
w the Universe Works" and documentaries on planets and their moons. Callisto, a moon of
er, was really fascinating. It went from there... I started writing in Cooper's voice:

as just a matter of chance that I became involved in the funeral biz. I wanted to be a pilot
explore the stars and all that crap.

a lot of flying, not a lot of exploring.

I dead bodies into space. That's my job now."

. The story grew from there. The future of funeral services smashed with a space horror/

en writing back and forth to artist, Steve Scott, and sent him the script. We'd worked
her before. I knew his style would be perfect. We talked to Sandy and sent her the idea.
oved it.

assembled a great team: Rodney Ramos on inks, Lovern Kindzierski on colors, and of
e, my frequent collaborator Janice Chiang on letters. We had our team and launched into
It was an enjoyable, smooth process and I couldn't be happier with the results. I hope you

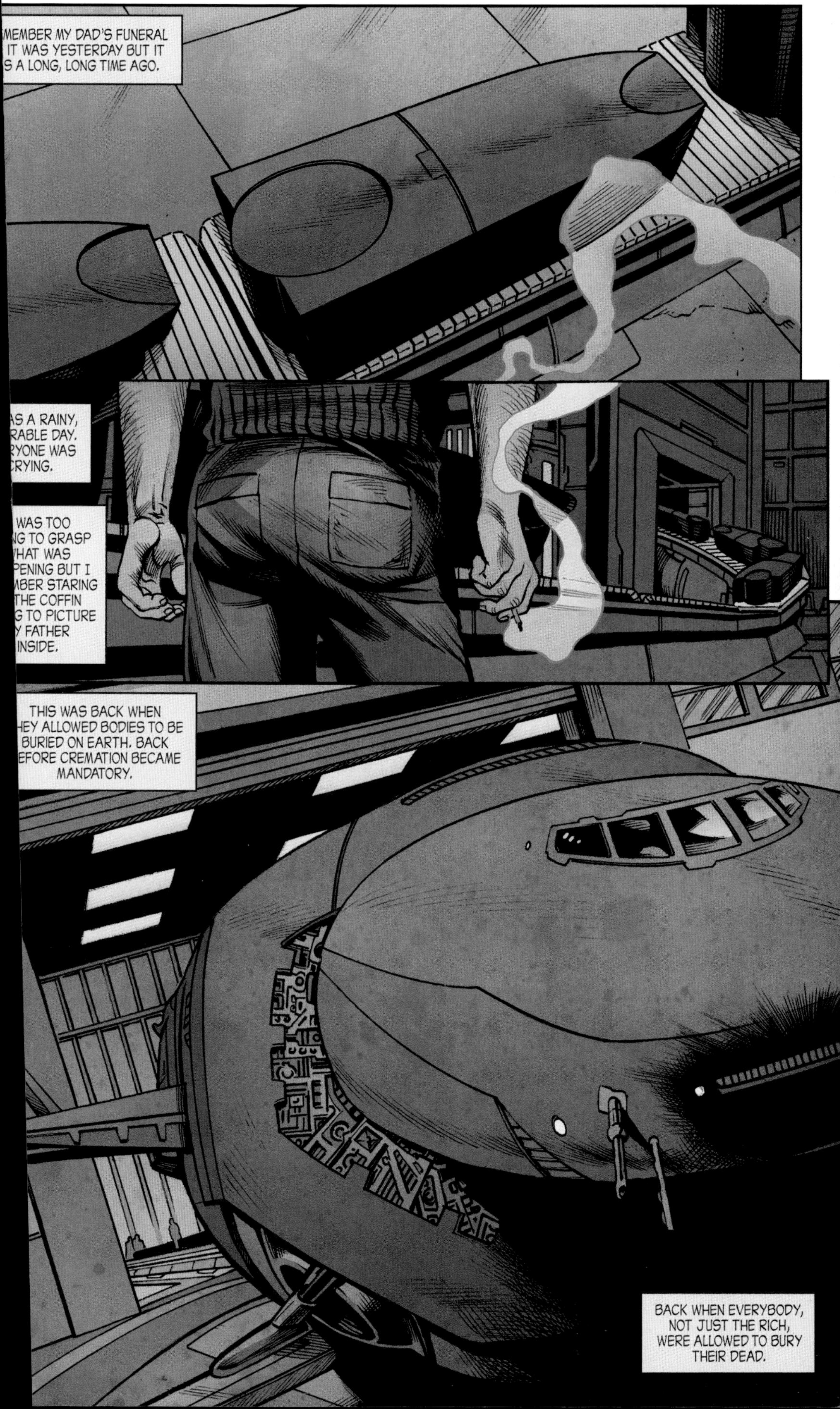
MEMBER MY DAD'S FUNERAL
IT WAS YESTERDAY BUT IT
S A LONG, LONG TIME AGO.
AS A RAINY,
RABLE DAY.
RYONE WAS
CRYING.
WAS TOO
NG TO GRASP
WHAT WAS
PENING BUT I
MBER STARING
THE COFFIN
G TO PICTURE
Y FATHER
INSIDE.
THIS WAS BACK WHEN
HEY ALLOWED BODIES TO BE
BURIED ON EARTH. BACK
EFORE CREMATION BECAME
MANDATORY.
BACK WHEN EVERYBODY,
NOT JUST THE RICH,
WERE ALLOWED TO BURY
THEIR DEAD.

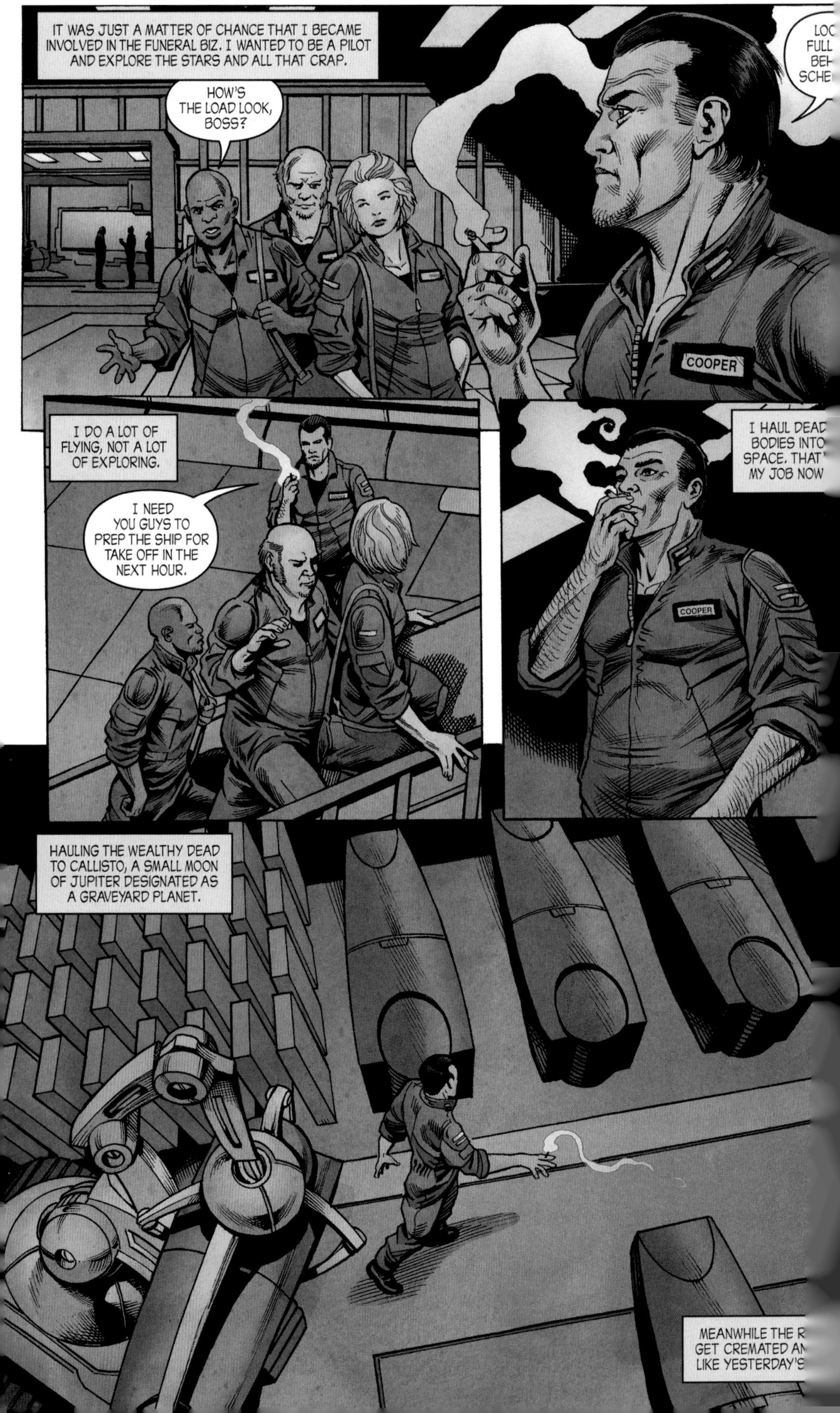

IT WAS JUST A MATTER OF CHANCE THAT I BECAME INVOLVED IN THE FUNERAL BIZ. I WANTED TO BE A PILOT AND EXPLORE THE STARS AND ALL THAT CRAP.
HOW'S THE LOAD LOOK, BOSS?
COOPER
I DO A LOT OF FLYING, NOT A LOT OF EXPLORING.
I NEED YOU GUYS TO PREP THE SHIP FOR TAKE OFF IN THE NEXT HOUR.
COOPER
HAULING THE WEALTHY DEAD TO CALLISTO, A SMALL MOON OF JUPITER DESIGNATED AS A GRAVEYARD PLANET.

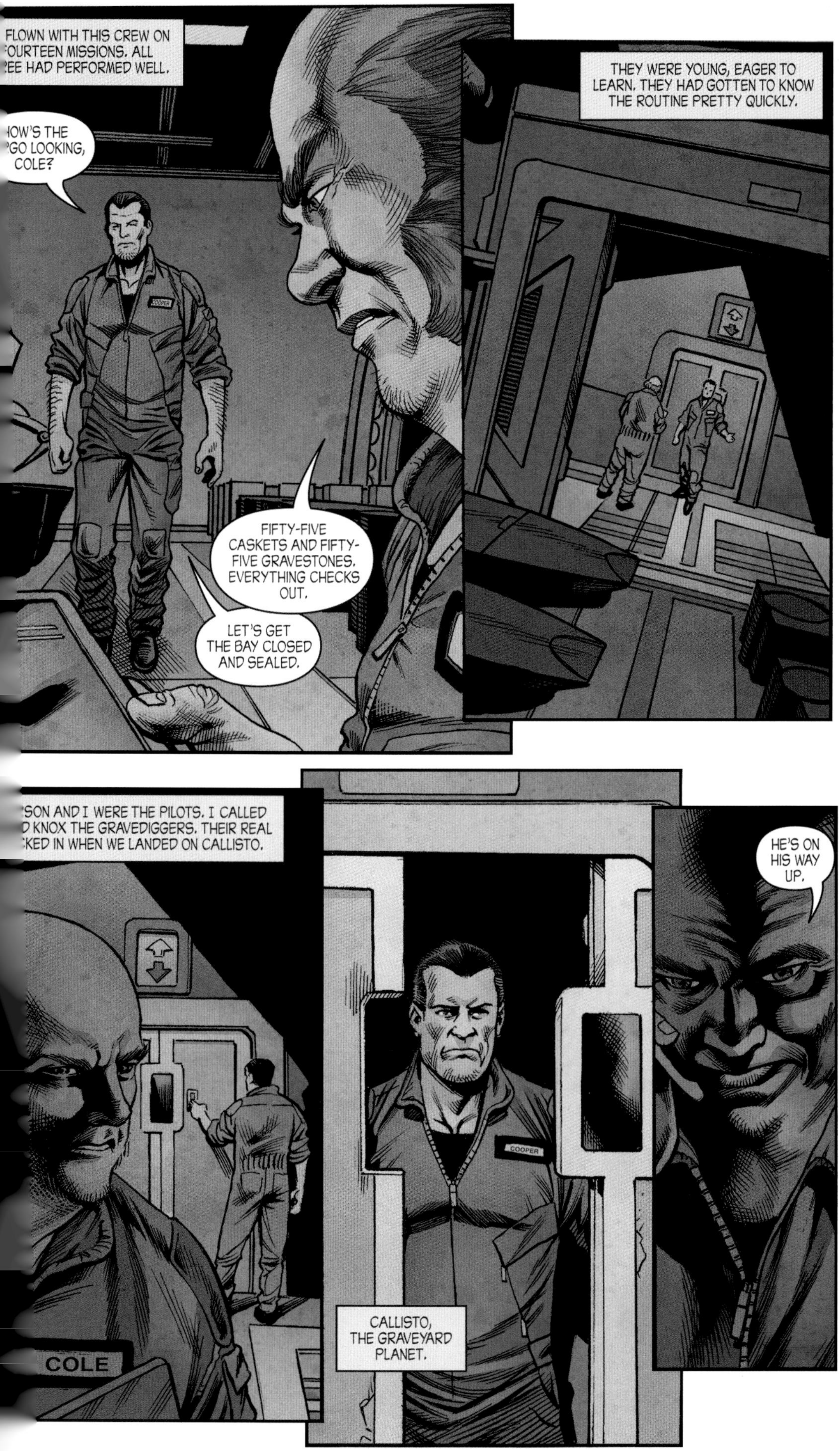
FLOWN WITH THIS CREW ON
OURTEEN MISSIONS. ALL
EE HAD PERFORMED WELL.
OW'S THE
GO LOOKING,
COLE?
FIFTY-FIVE CASKETS AND FIFTY-FIVE GRAVESTONES. EVERYTHING CHECKS OUT.
LET'S GET THE BAY CLOSED AND SEALED.
COOPER
THEY WERE YOUNG, EAGER TO LEARN. THEY HAD GOTTEN TO KNOW THE ROUTINE PRETTY QUICKLY.
SON AND I WERE THE PILOTS. I CALLED
D KNOX THE GRAVEDIGGERS. THEIR REAL
KED IN WHEN WE LANDED ON CALLISTO.
COLE
COOPER
CALLISTO, THE GRAVEYARD PLANET.
HE'S ON HIS WAY UP.

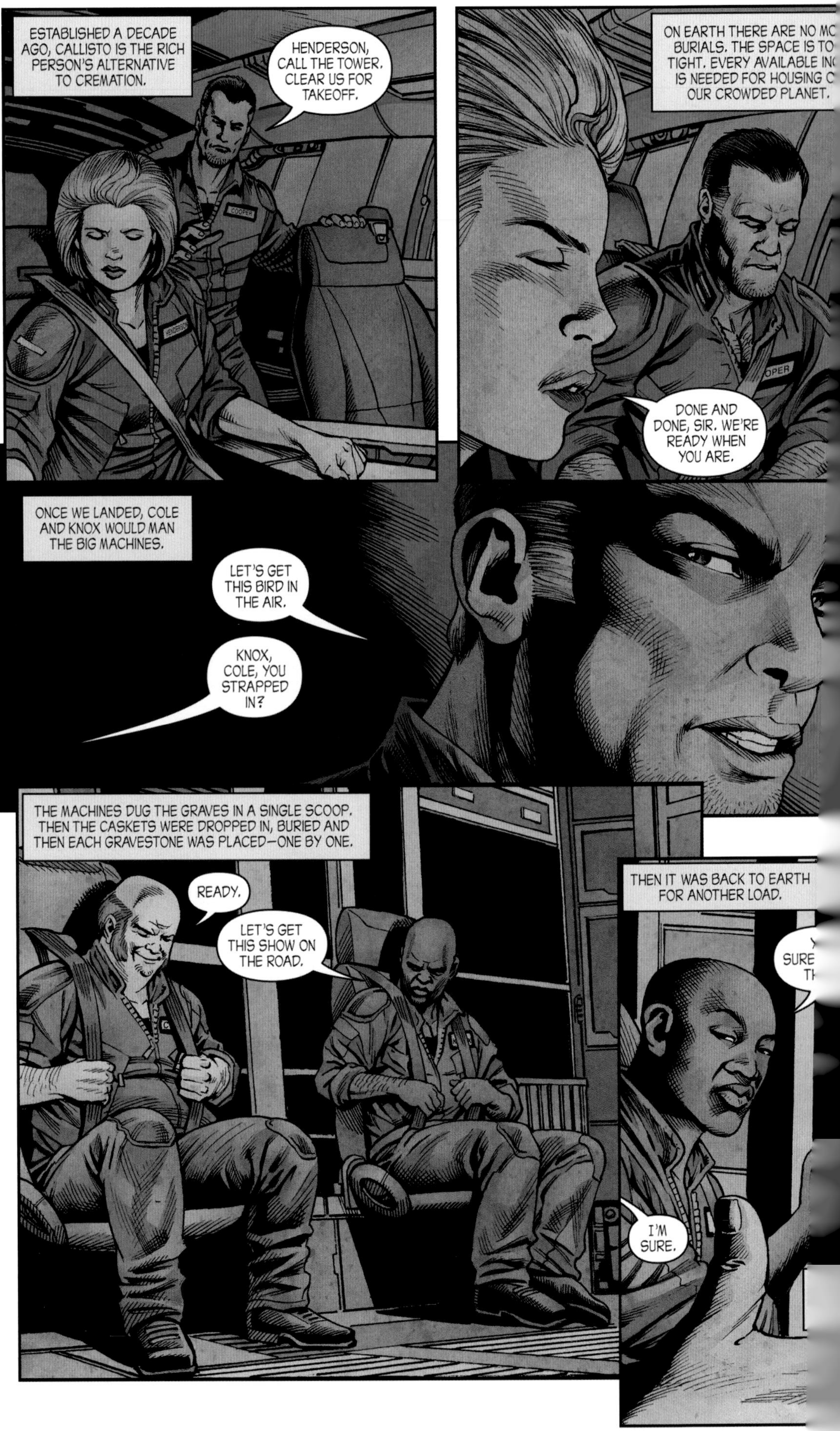
ESTABLISHED A DECADE AGO, CALLISTO IS THE RICH PERSON'S ALTERNATIVE TO CREMATION.
HENDERSON, CALL THE TOWER. CLEAR US FOR TAKEOFF.
ON EARTH THERE ARE NO MO BURIALS. THE SPACE IS TO TIGHT. EVERY AVAILABLE IN IS NEEDED FOR HOUSING O OUR CROWDED PLANET.
DONE AND DONE, SIR. WE'RE READY WHEN YOU ARE.
ONCE WE LANDED, COLE AND KNOX WOULD MAN THE BIG MACHINES.
LET'S GET THIS BIRD IN THE AIR.
KNOX, COLE, YOU STRAPPED IN?
THE MACHINES DUG THE GRAVES IN A SINGLE SCOOP. THEN THE CASKETS WERE DROPPED IN, BURIED AND THEN EACH GRAVESTONE WAS PLACED—ONE BY ONE.
READY.
LET'S GET THIS SHOW ON THE ROAD.
THEN IT WAS BACK TO EARTH FOR ANOTHER LOAD.
I'M SURE.

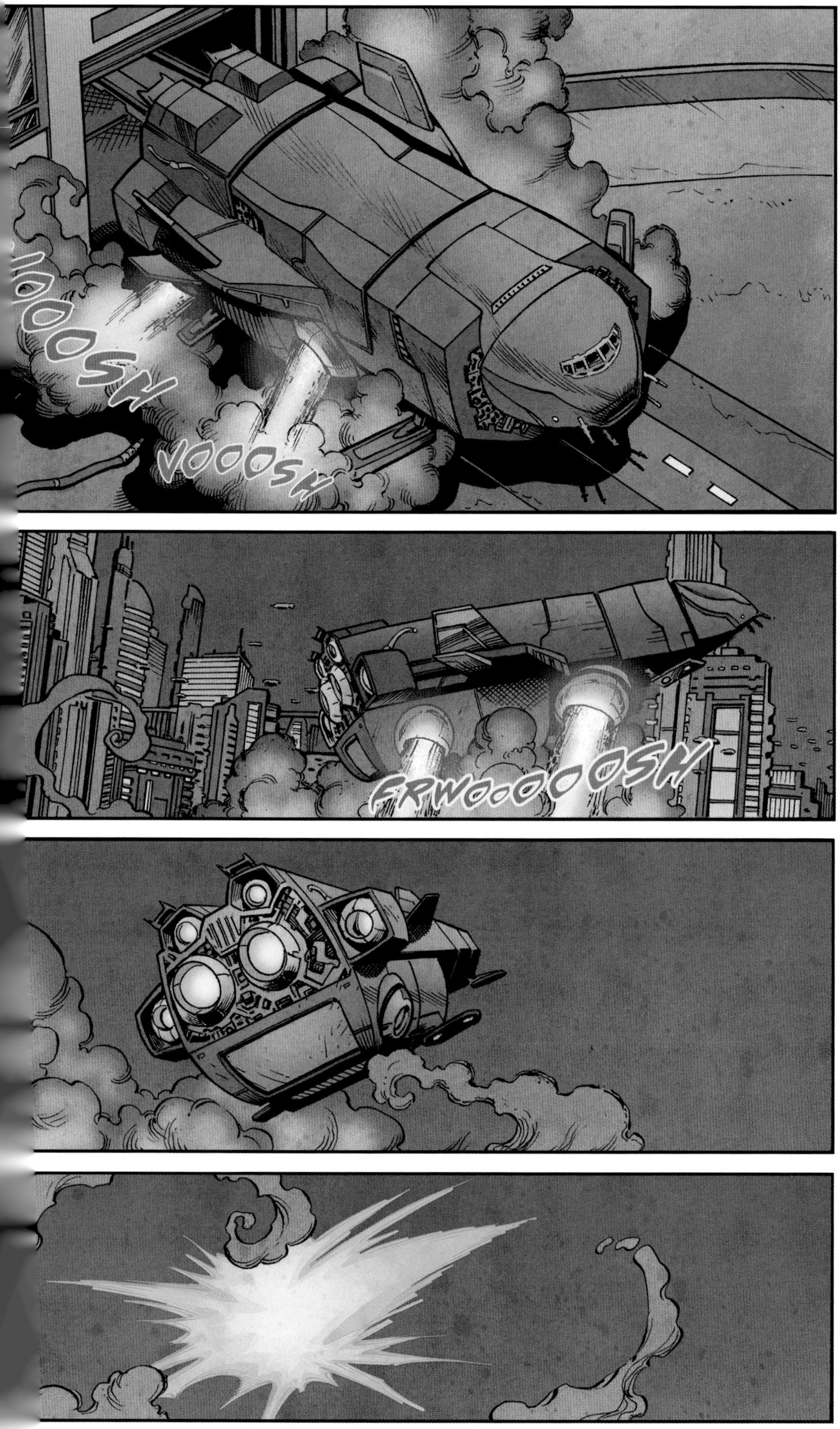
OOOSH
VOOOSH
FRWO-OOOOSH

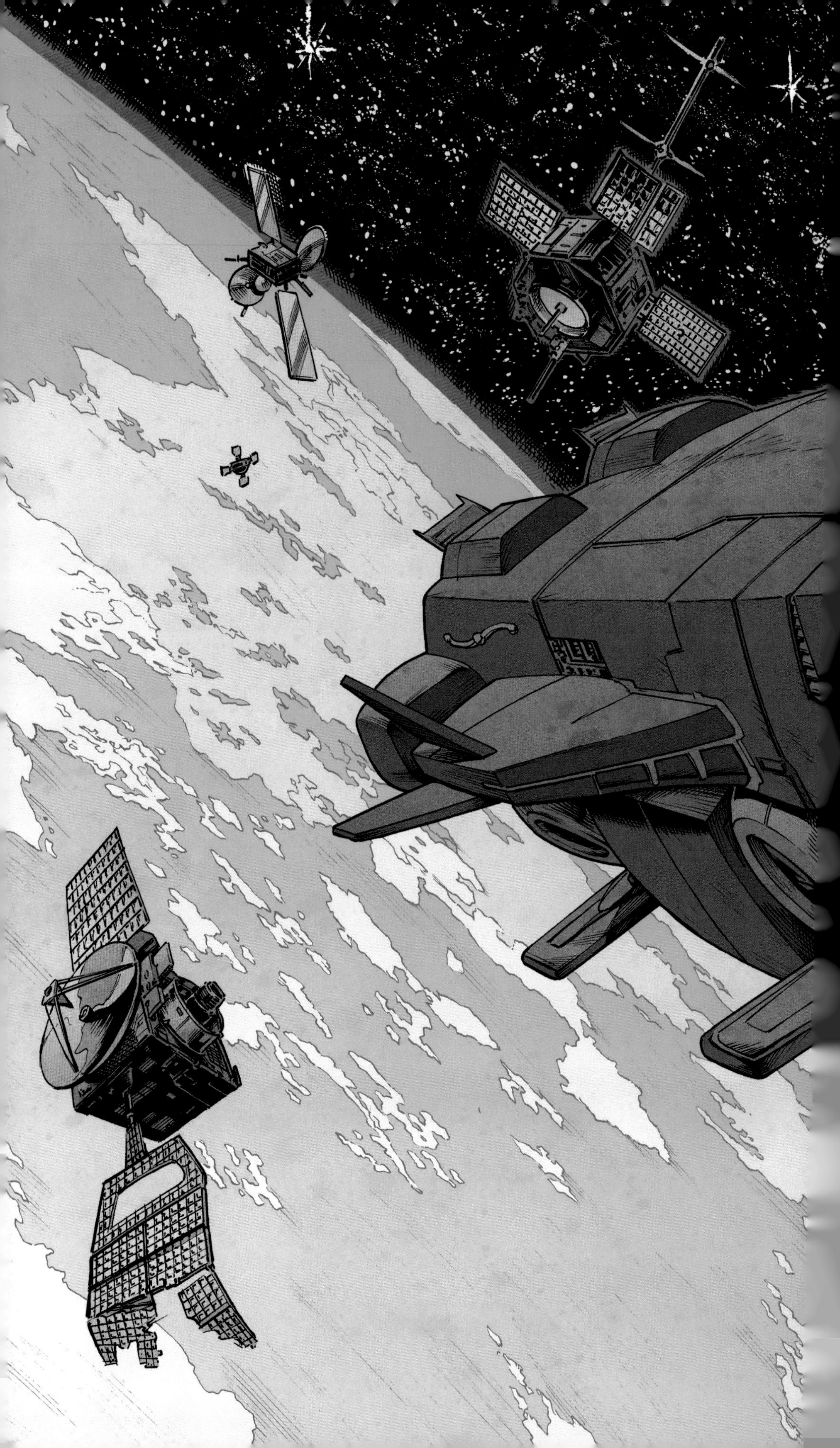

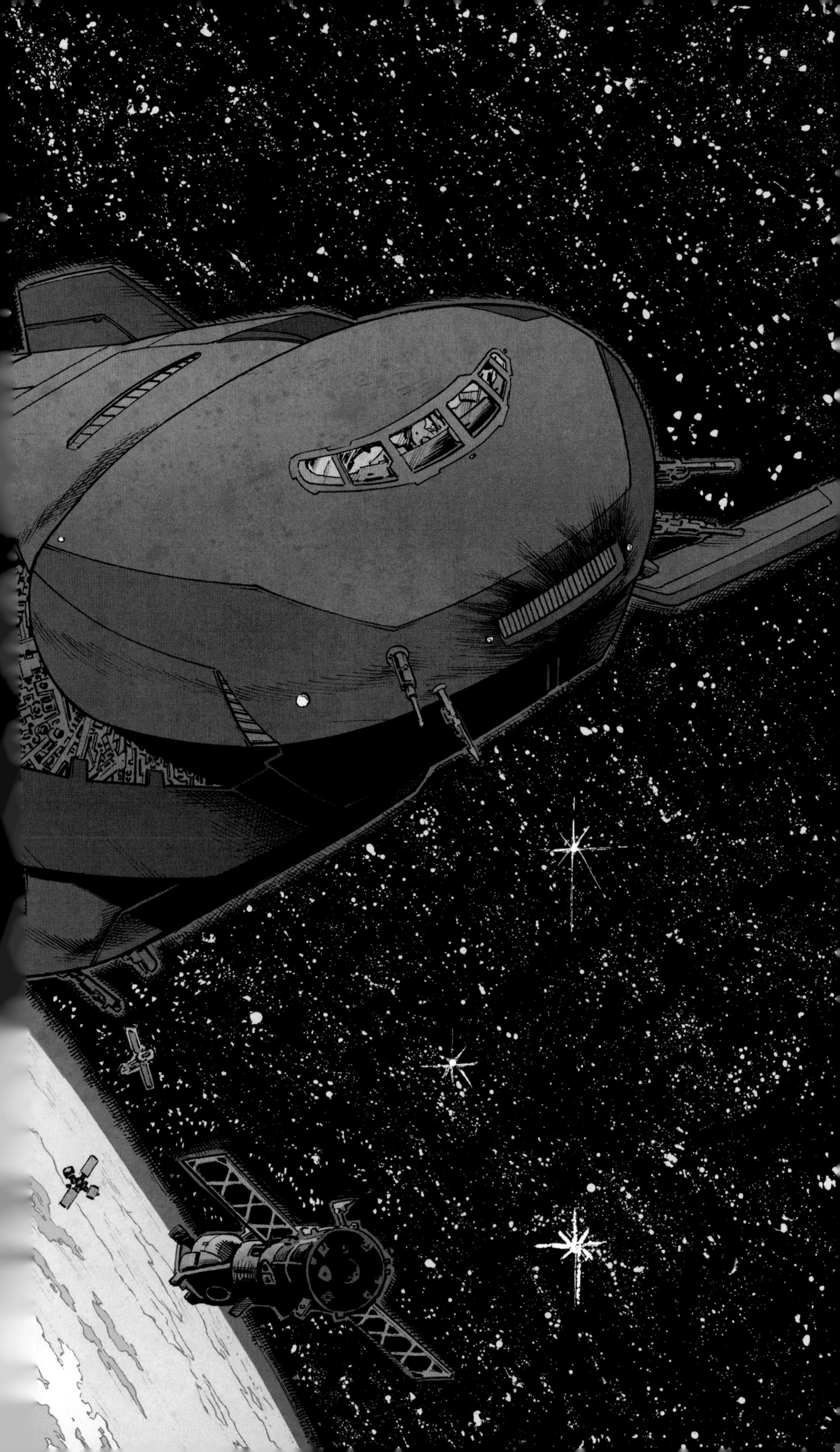

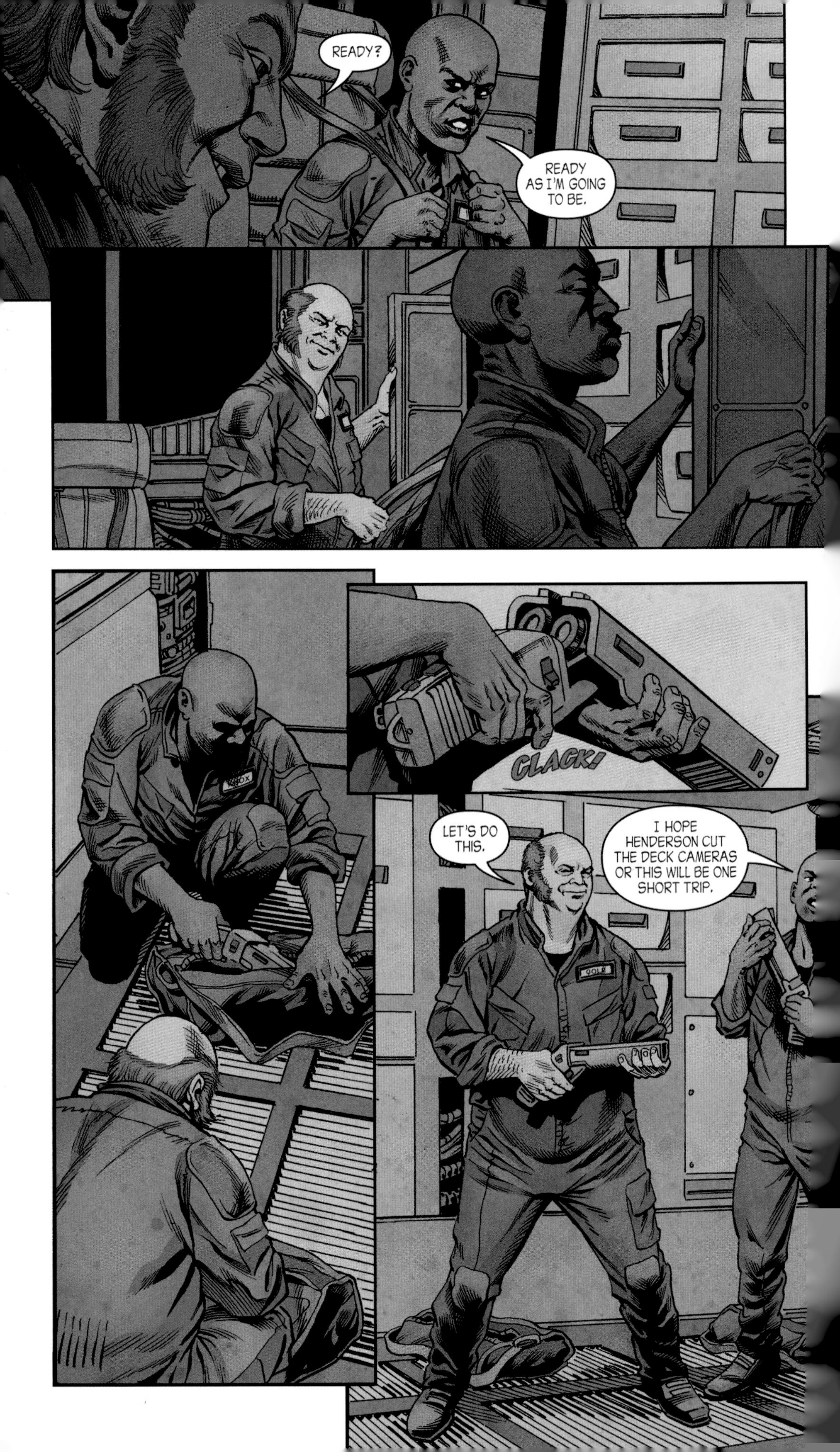
READY?
READY AS I'M GOING TO BE.
CLACK!
LET'S DO THIS.
I HOPE HENDERSON CUT THE DECK CAMERAS OR THIS WILL BE ONE SHORT TRIP.

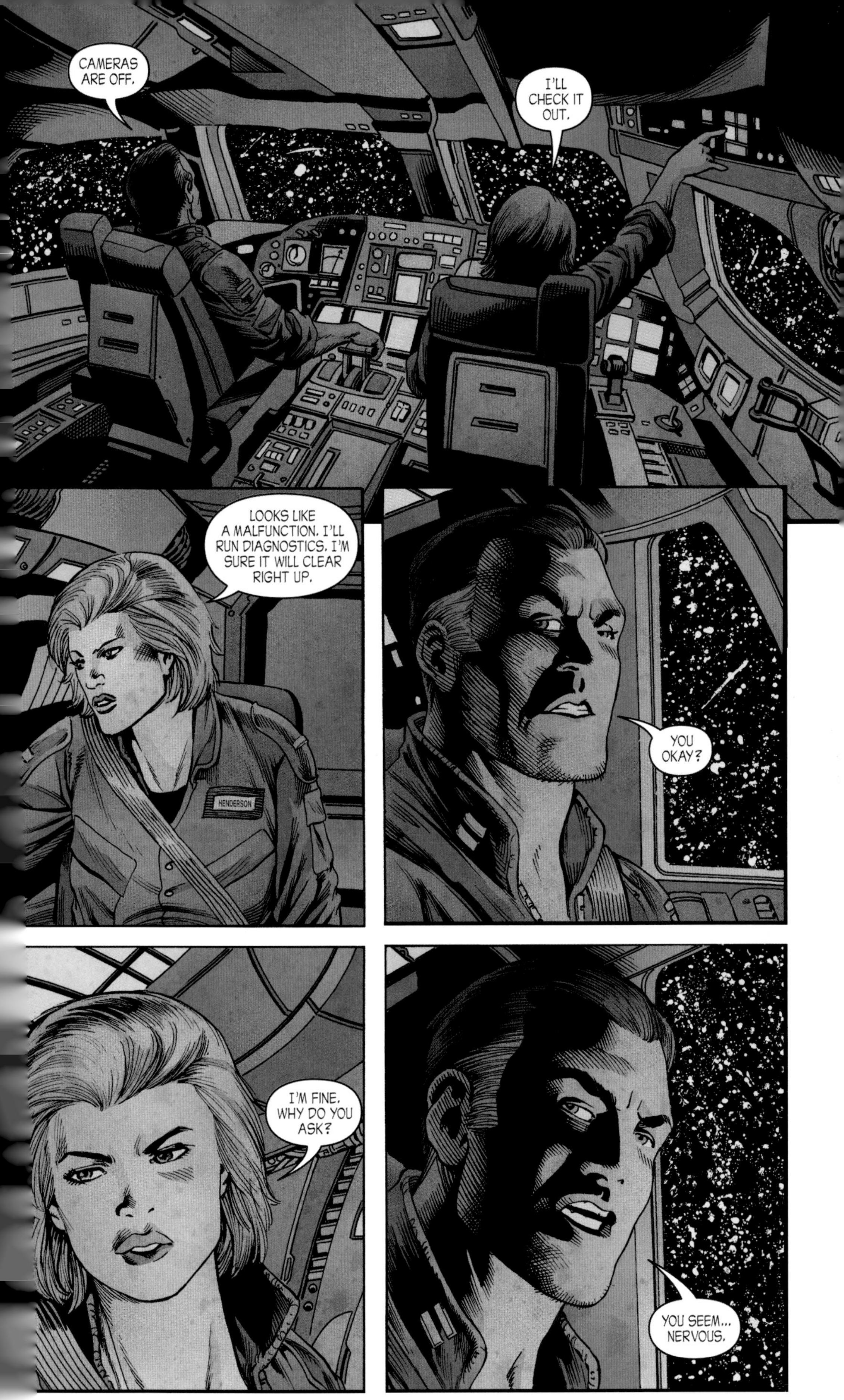
CAMERAS ARE OFF.
I'LL CHECK IT OUT.
LOOKS LIKE A MALFUNCTION. I'LL RUN DIAGNOSTICS. I'M SURE IT WILL CLEAR RIGHT UP.
HENDERSON
YOU OKAY?
I'M FINE. WHY DO YOU ASK?
YOU SEEM... NERVOUS.

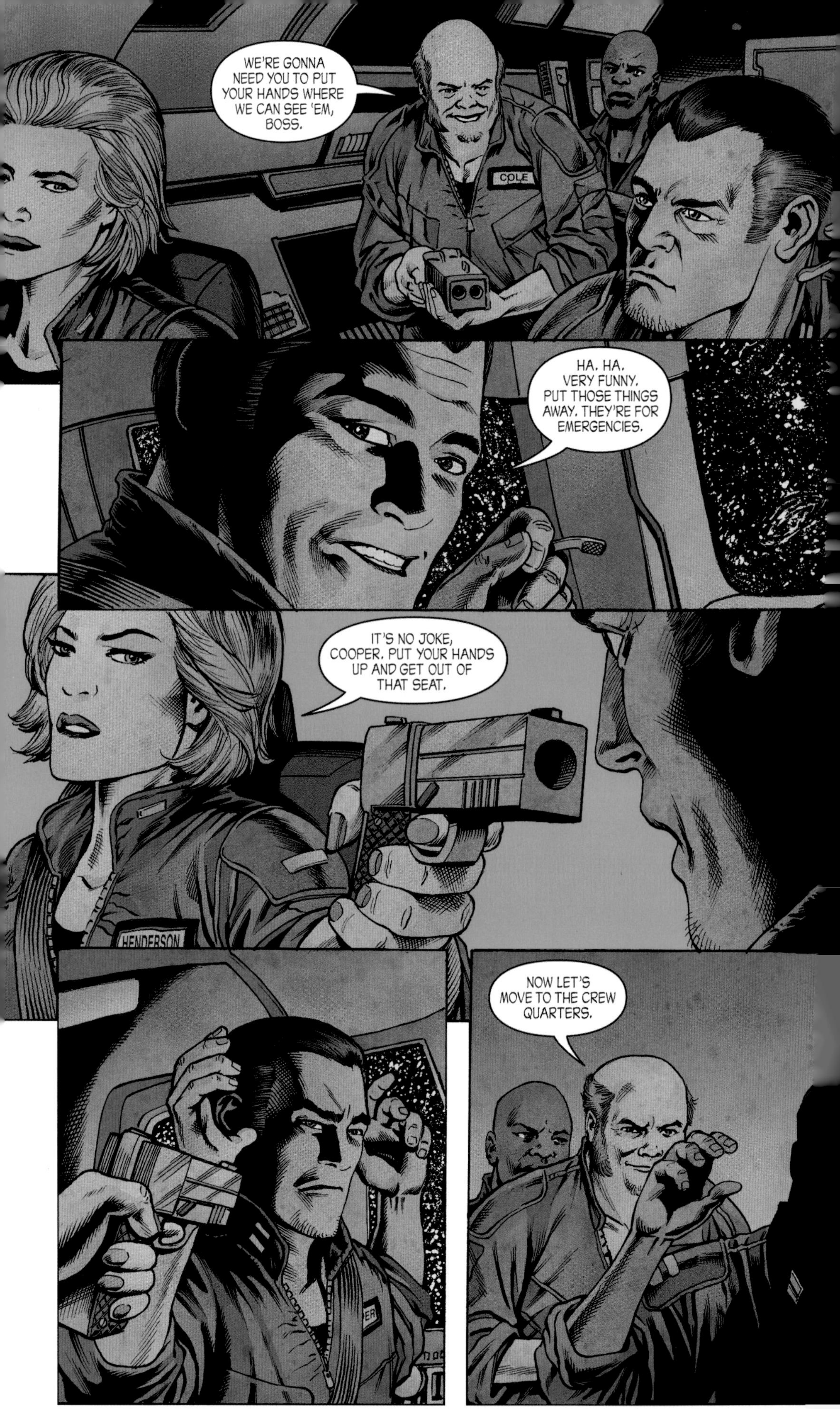
WE'RE GONNA NEED YOU TO PUT YOUR HANDS WHERE WE CAN SEE 'EM, BOSS.
COLE
HA. HA. VERY FUNNY. PUT THOSE THINGS AWAY. THEY'RE FOR EMERGENCIES.
IT'S NO JOKE, COOPER. PUT YOUR HANDS UP AND GET OUT OF THAT SEAT.
HENDERSON
NOW LET'S MOVE TO THE CREW QUARTERS.

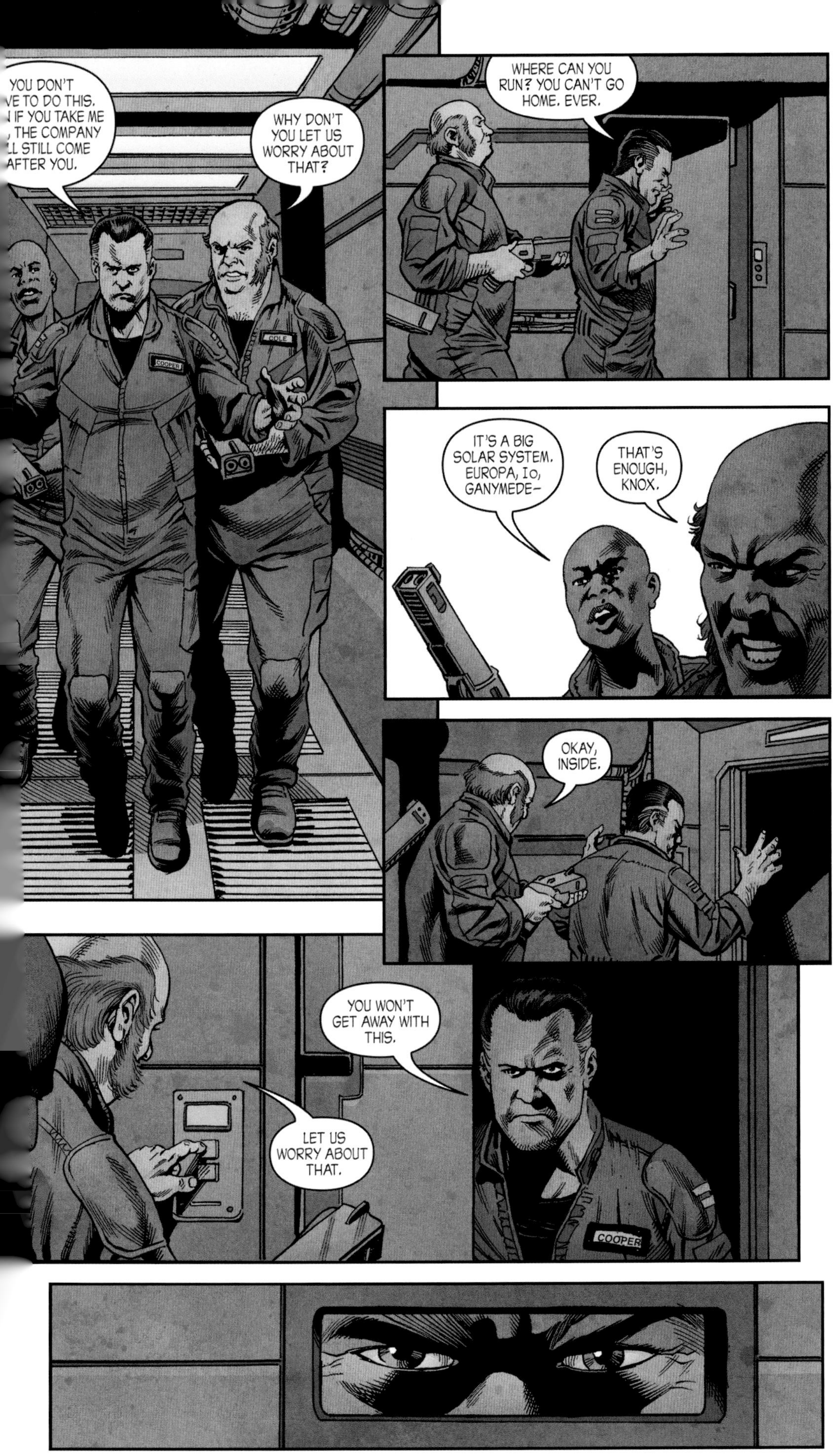
YOU DON'T VE TO DO THIS. I IF YOU TAKE ME , THE COMPANY LL STILL COME AFTER YOU.
WHY DON'T YOU LET US WORRY ABOUT THAT?
WHERE CAN YOU RUN? YOU CAN'T GO HOME. EVER.
COOPER
COLE
IT'S A BIG SOLAR SYSTEM. EUROPA, Io, GANYMEDE-
THAT'S ENOUGH, KNOX.
OKAY, INSIDE.
YOU WON'T GET AWAY WITH THIS.
LET US WORRY ABOUT THAT.
COOPER

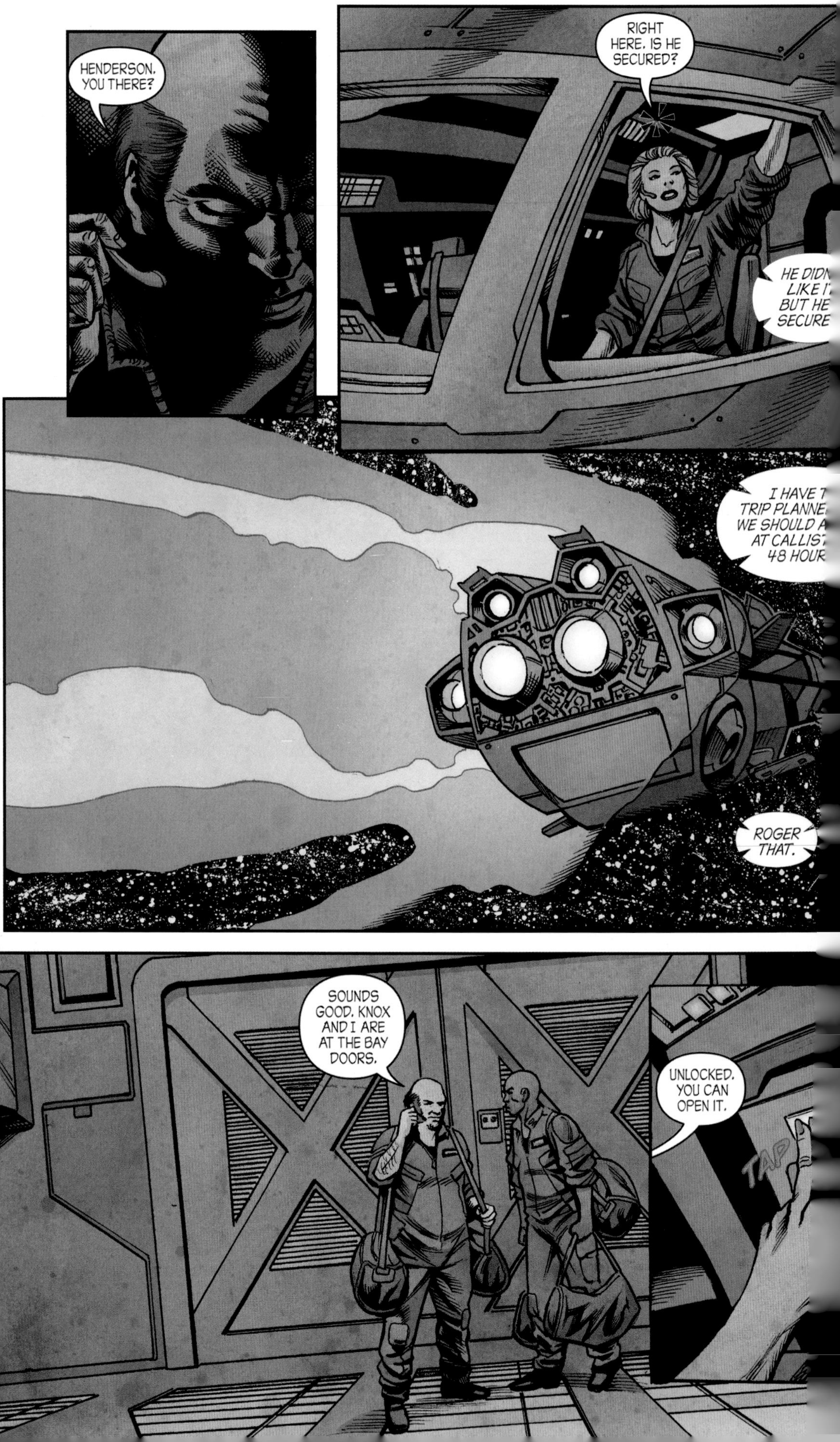
HENDERSON. YOU THERE?
RIGHT HERE. IS HE SECURED?
HE DIDN LIKE I BUT HE SECURE
I HAVE T TRIP PLANNE WE SHOULD A AT CALLIST 48 HOUR
ROGER THAT.
SOUNDS GOOD. KNOX AND I ARE AT THE BAY DOORS.
UNLOCKED. YOU CAN OPEN IT.
TAP

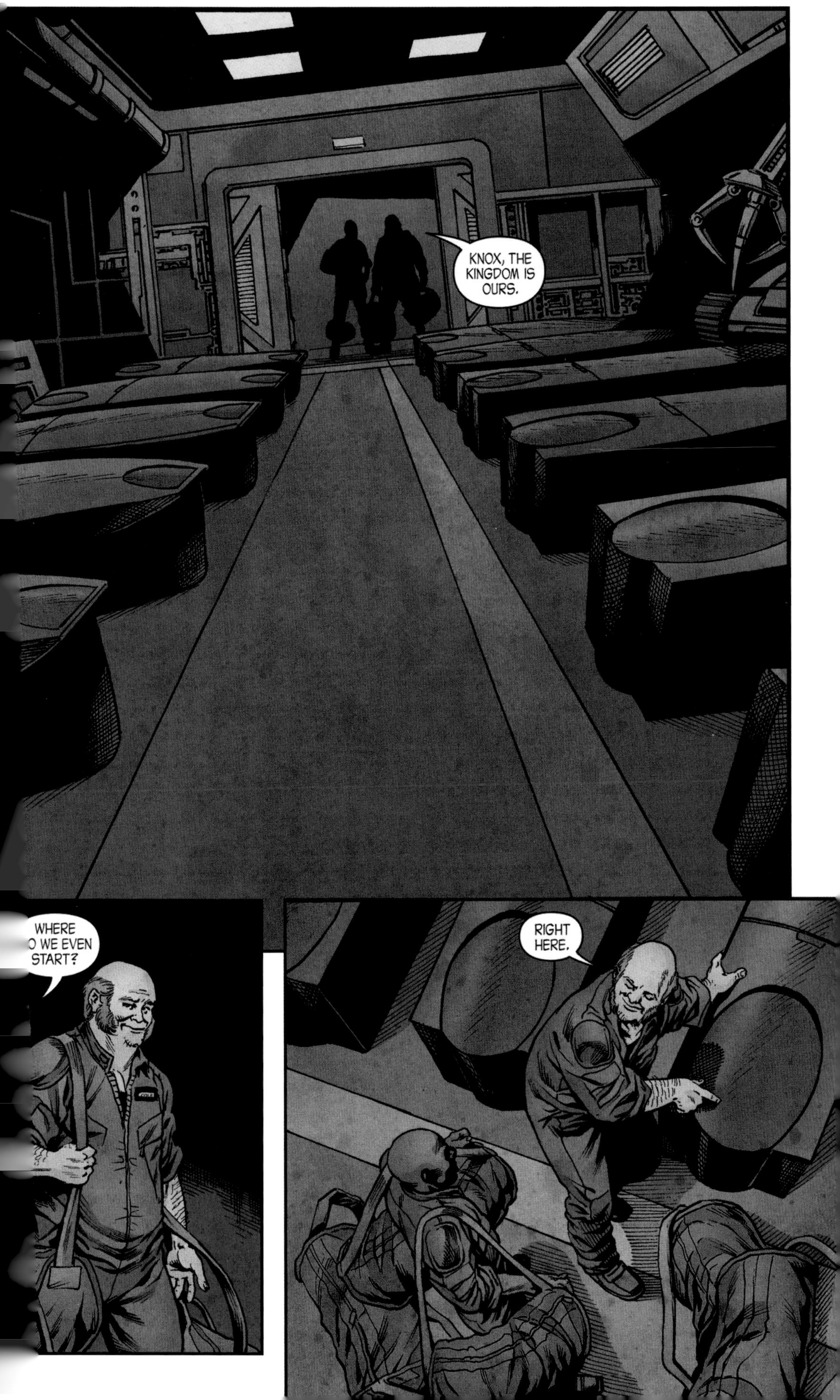
KNOX, THE KINGDOM IS OURS.
WHERE O WE EVEN START?
RIGHT HERE.

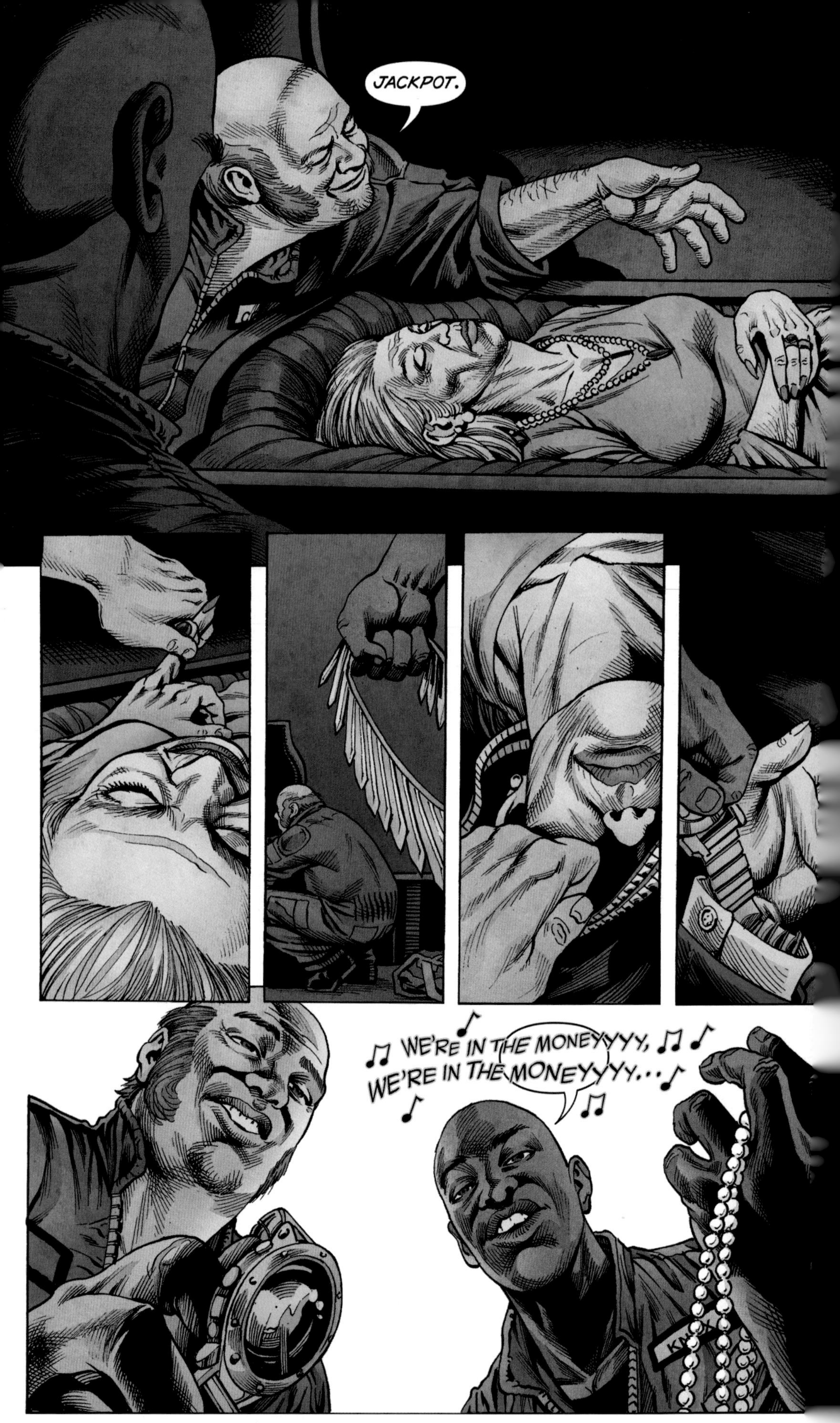
JACKPOT.
♫ WE'RE IN THE MONEYYYY, ♫ ♪
WE'RE IN THE MONEYYYY... ♪
♪ ♫

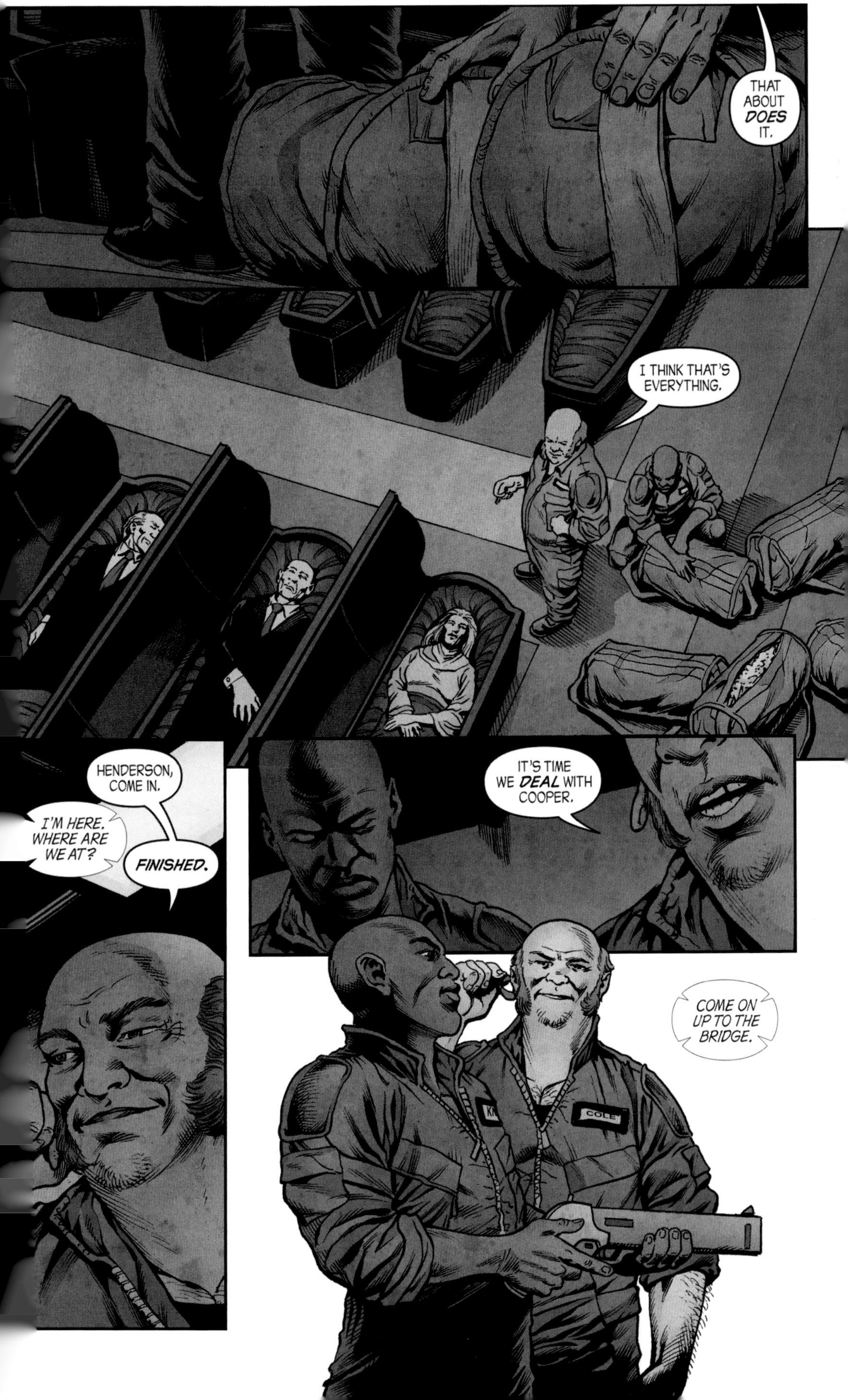

THAT ABOUT DOES IT.
I THINK THAT'S EVERYTHING.
HENDERSON, COME IN.
I'M HERE. WHERE ARE WE AT?
FINISHED.
IT'S TIME WE DEAL WITH COOPER.
COME ON UP TO THE BRIDGE.
COLE

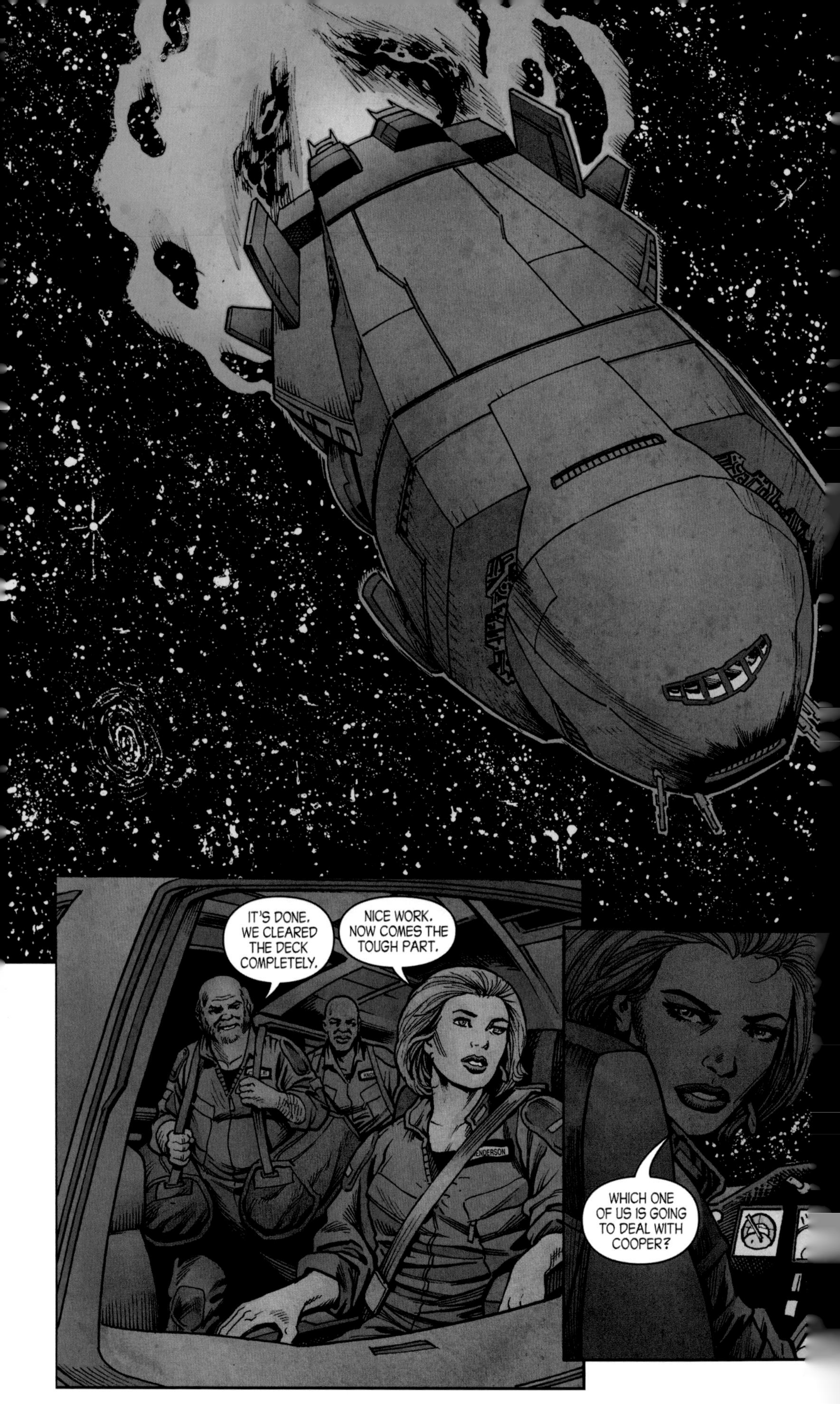
IT'S DONE. WE CLEARED THE DECK COMPLETELY.
NICE WORK. NOW COMES THE TOUGH PART.
WHICH ONE OF US IS GOING TO DEAL WITH COOPER?

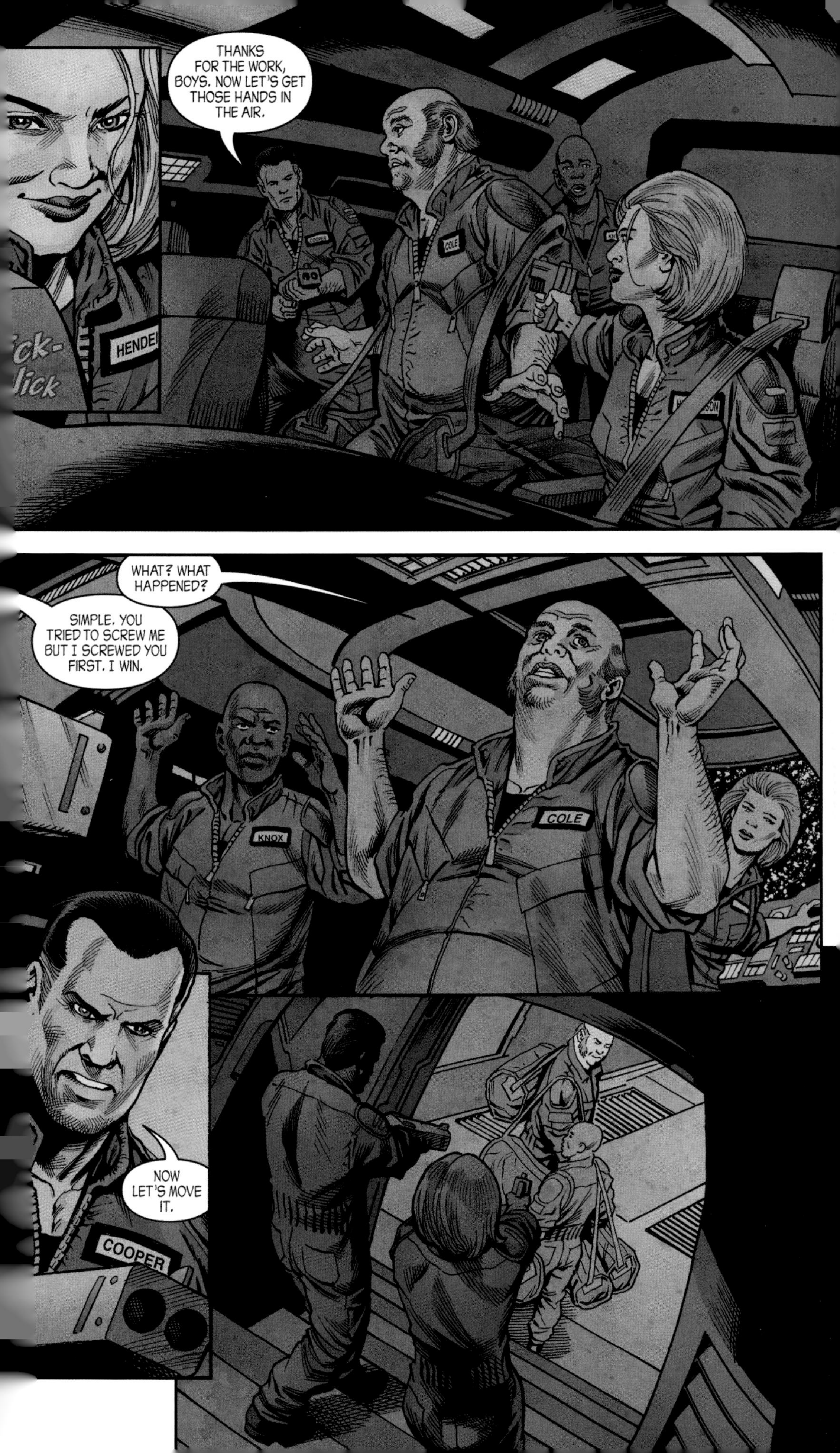
THANKS FOR THE WORK, BOYS. NOW LET'S GET THOSE HANDS IN THE AIR.
WHAT? WHAT HAPPENED?
SIMPLE. YOU TRIED TO SCREW ME BUT I SCREWED YOU FIRST. I WIN.
NOW LET'S MOVE IT.

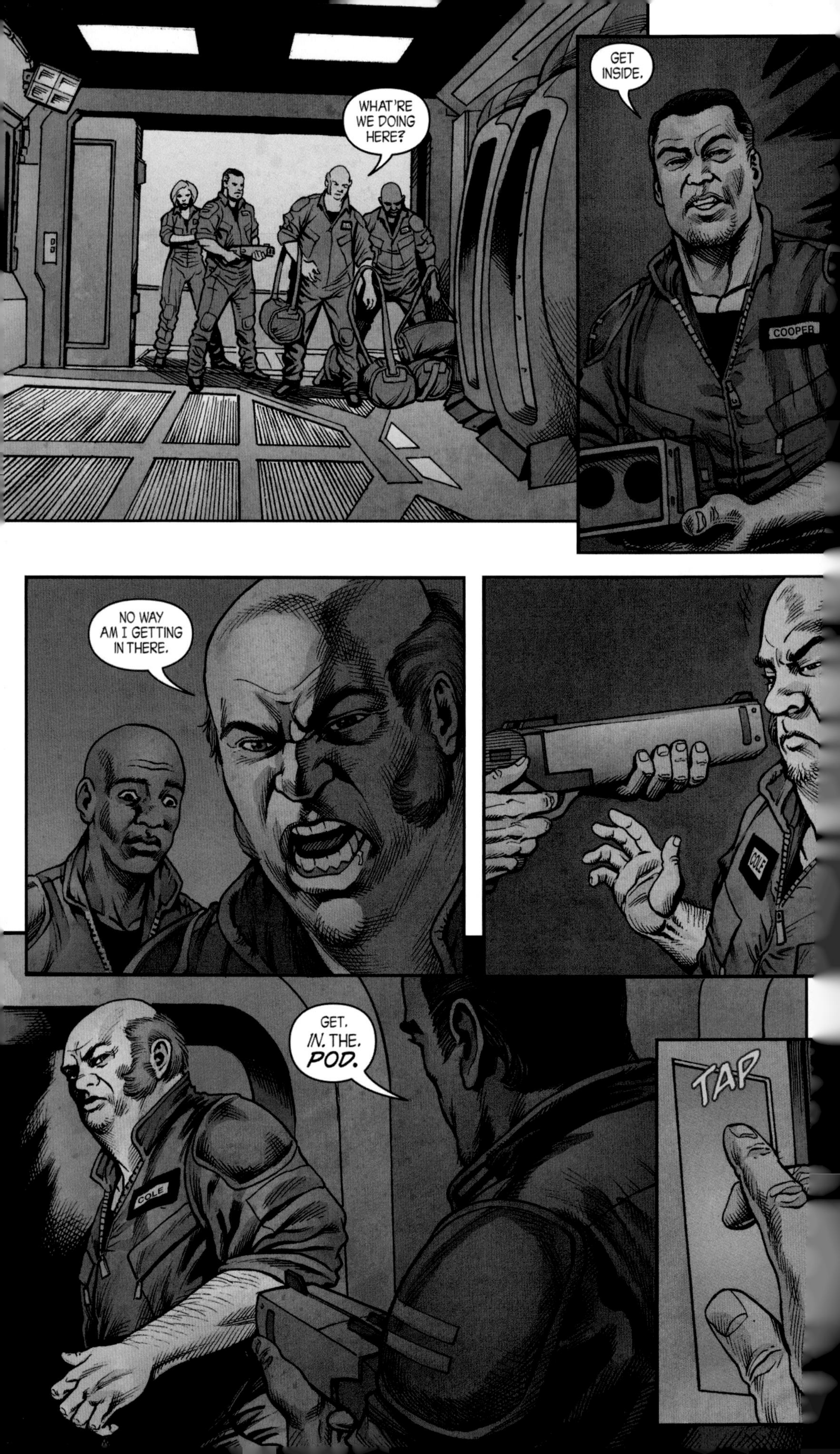
WHAT'RE WE DOING HERE?
GET INSIDE.
COOPER
NO WAY AM I GETTING IN THERE.
COLE
GET. *IN.* THE. ***POD.***
COLE
TAP

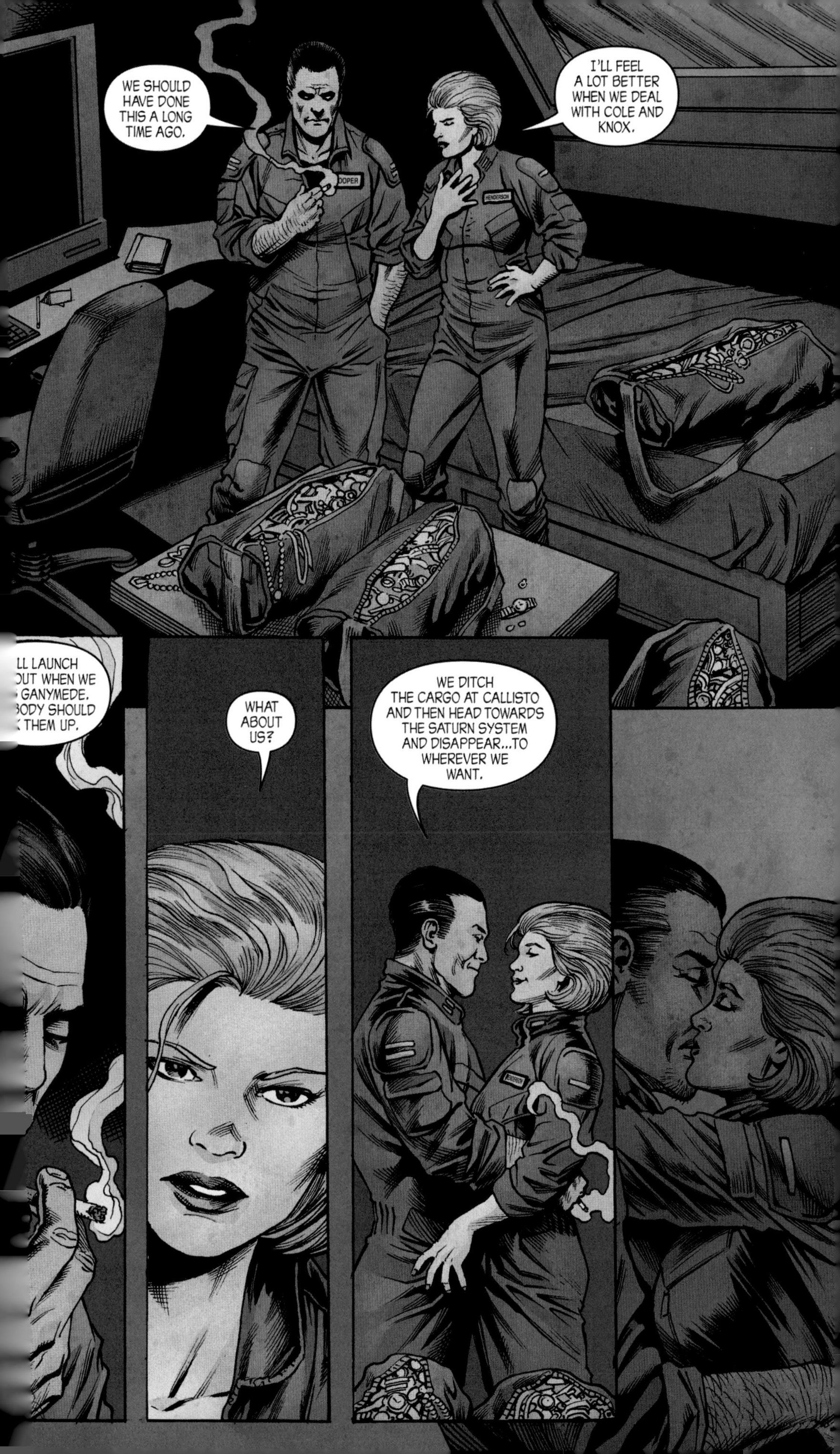

WE SHOULD HAVE DONE THIS A LONG TIME AGO.
I'LL FEEL A LOT BETTER WHEN WE DEAL WITH COLE AND KNOX.
LL LAUNCH OUT WHEN WE GANYMEDE. BODY SHOULD THEM UP.
WHAT ABOUT US?
WE DITCH THE CARGO AT CALLISTO AND THEN HEAD TOWARDS THE SATURN SYSTEM AND DISAPPEAR...TO WHEREVER WE WANT.

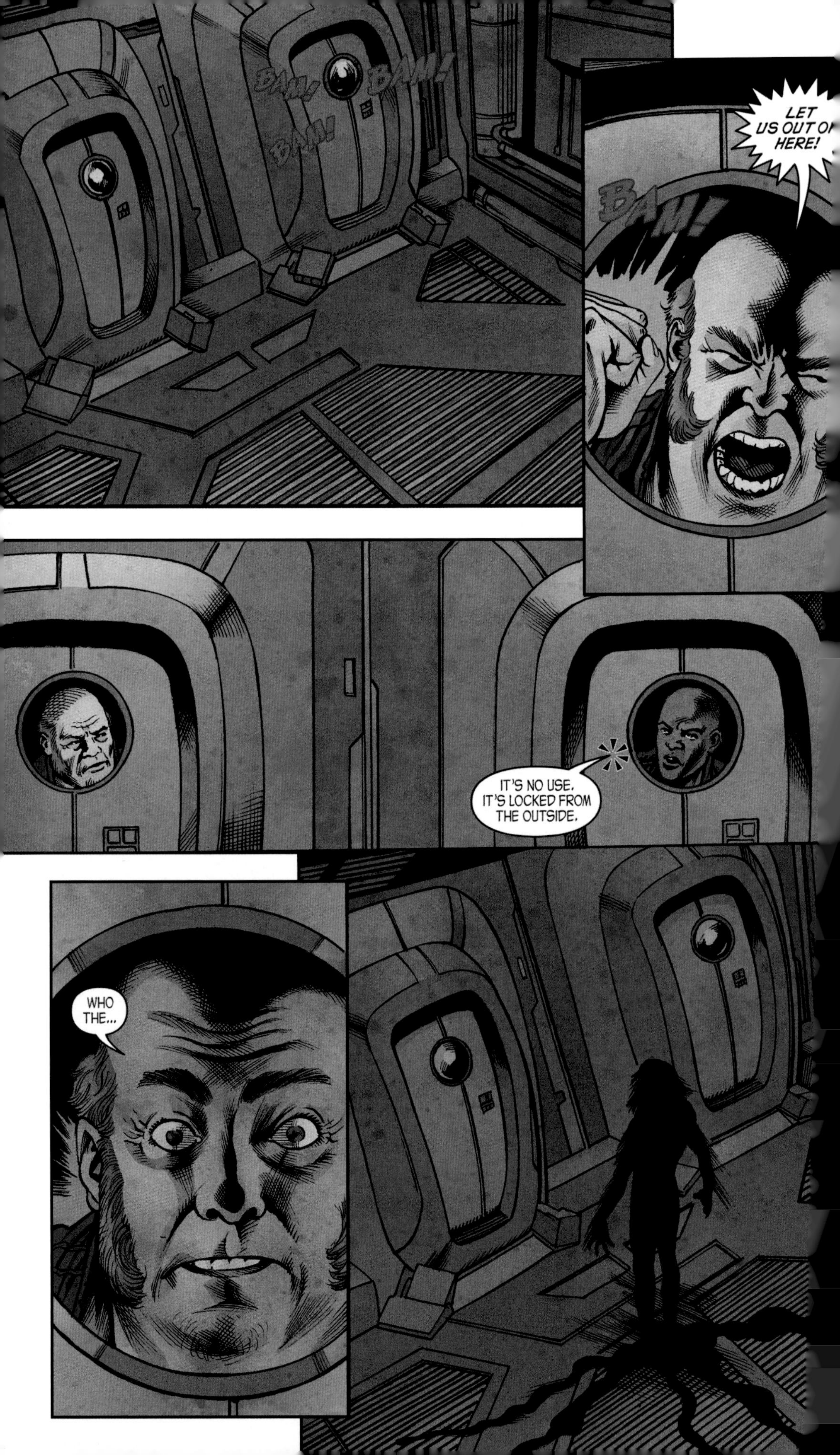
BAM! BAM!
BAM!
LET US OUT OF HERE!
BAM!
IT'S NO USE. IT'S LOCKED FROM THE OUTSIDE.
WHO THE...

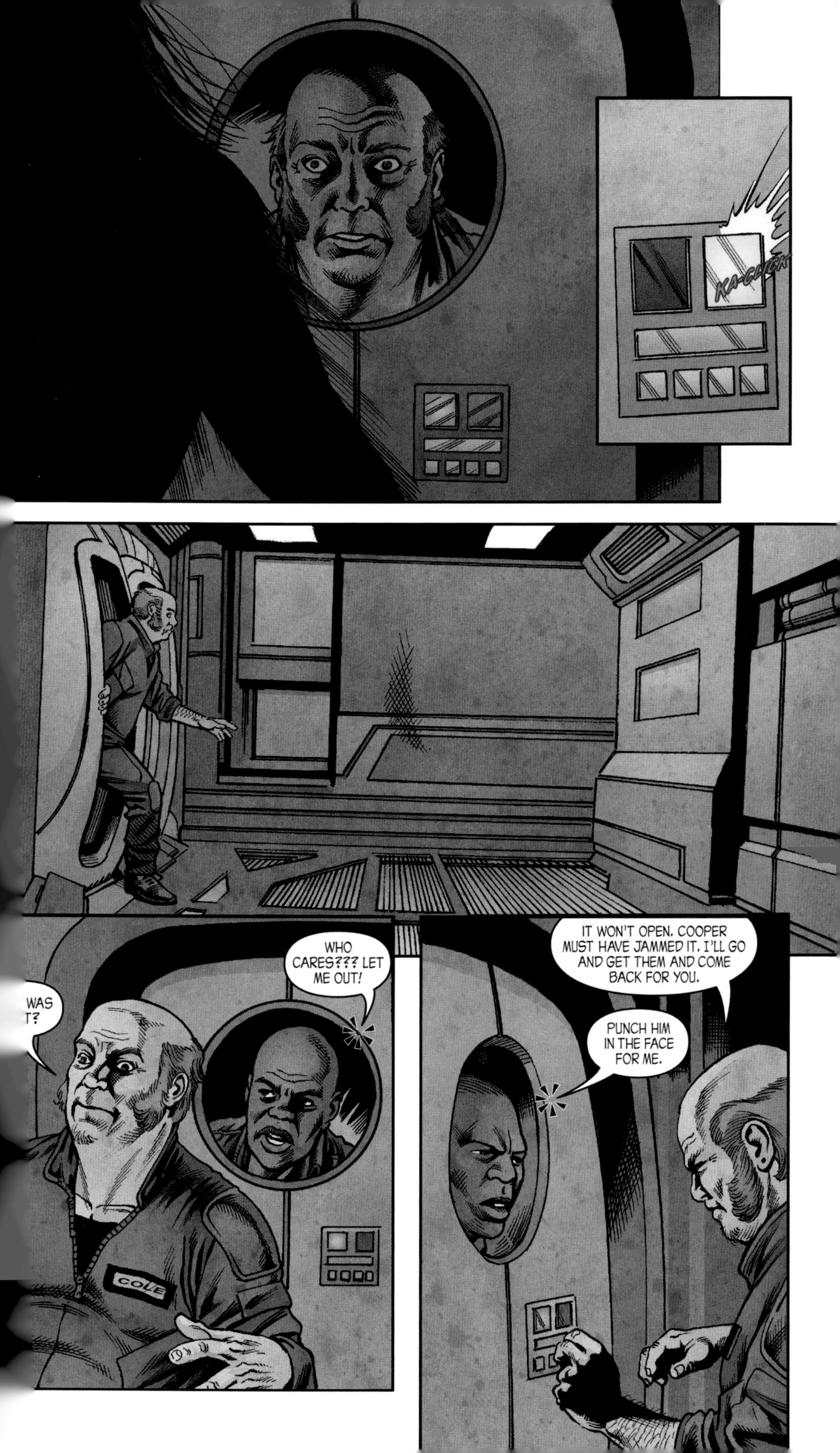
KA-CLICK
WAS
T?
WHO CARES??? LET ME OUT!
COLE
IT WON'T OPEN. COOPER MUST HAVE JAMMED IT. I'LL GO AND GET THEM AND COME BACK FOR YOU.
PUNCH HIM IN THE FACE FOR ME.

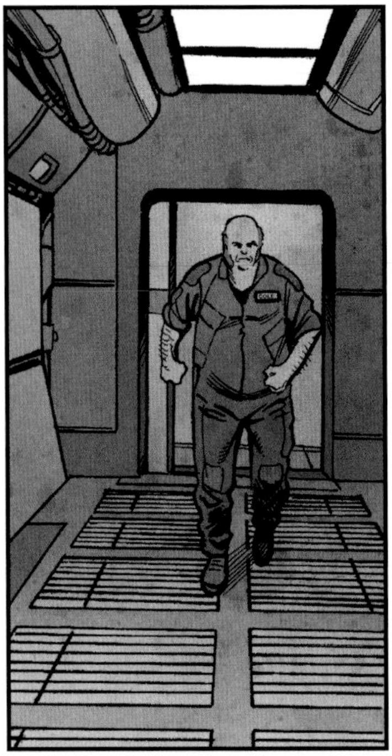
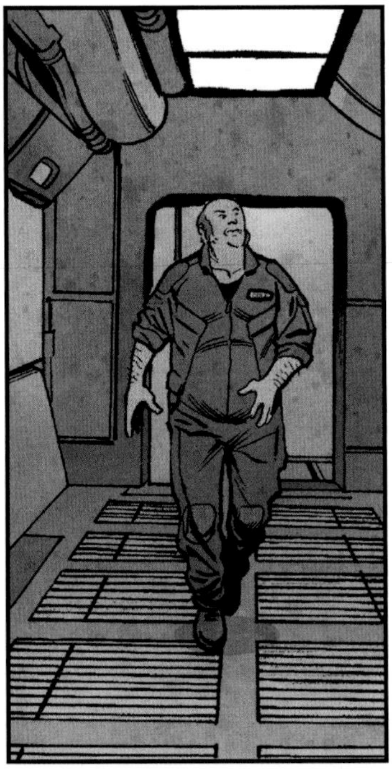
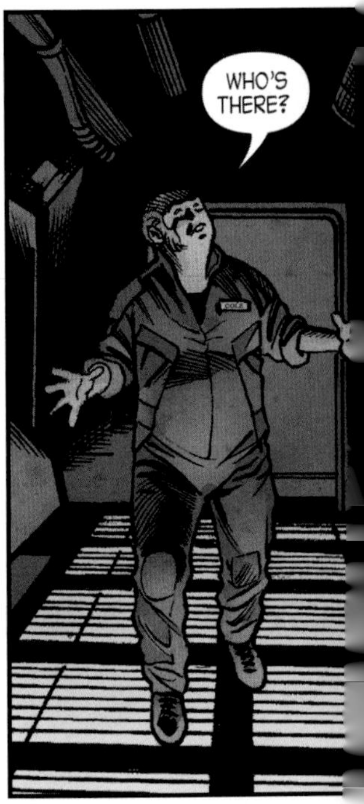
WHO'S THERE?
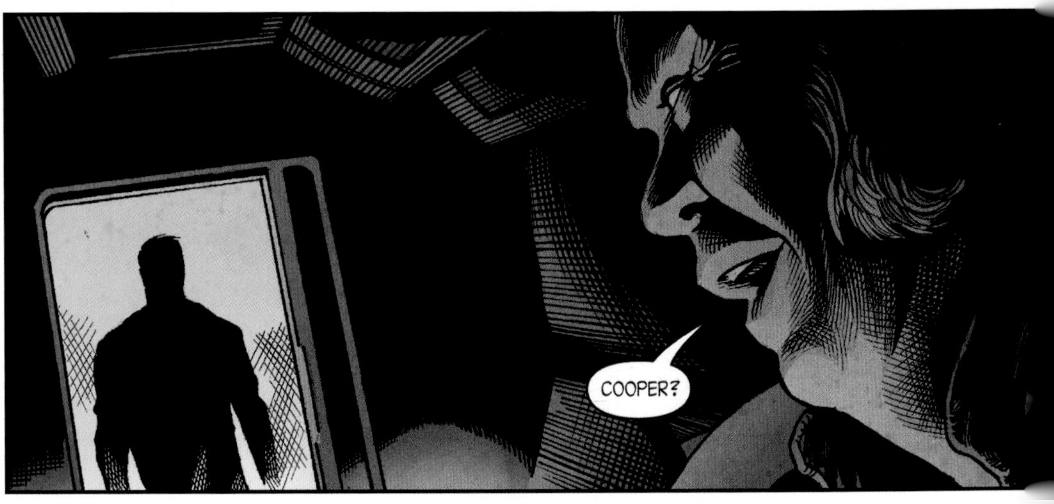
COOPER?
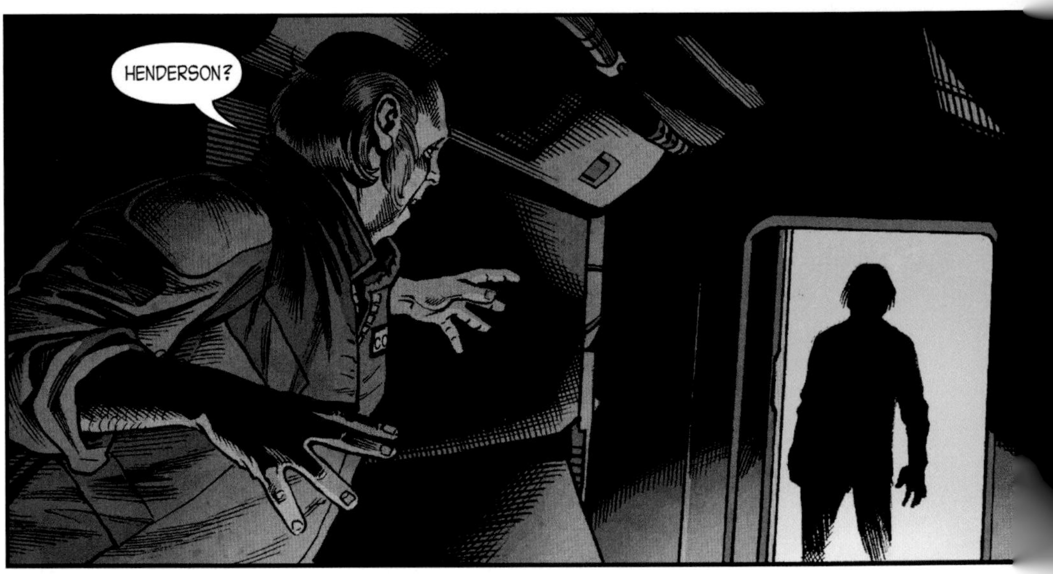
HENDERSON?

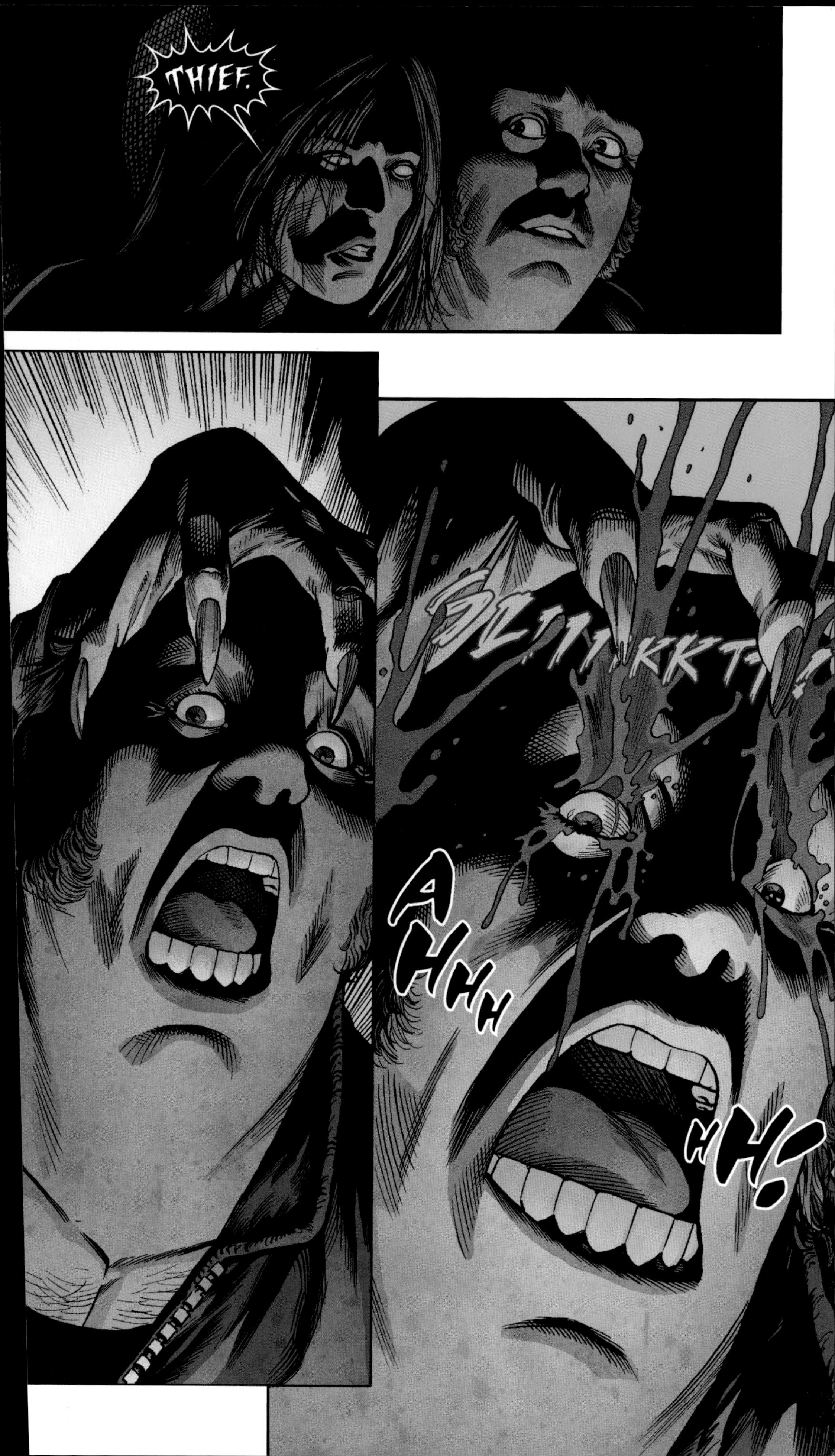
THIEF.
SLIIIKKT!
AHHHHH!

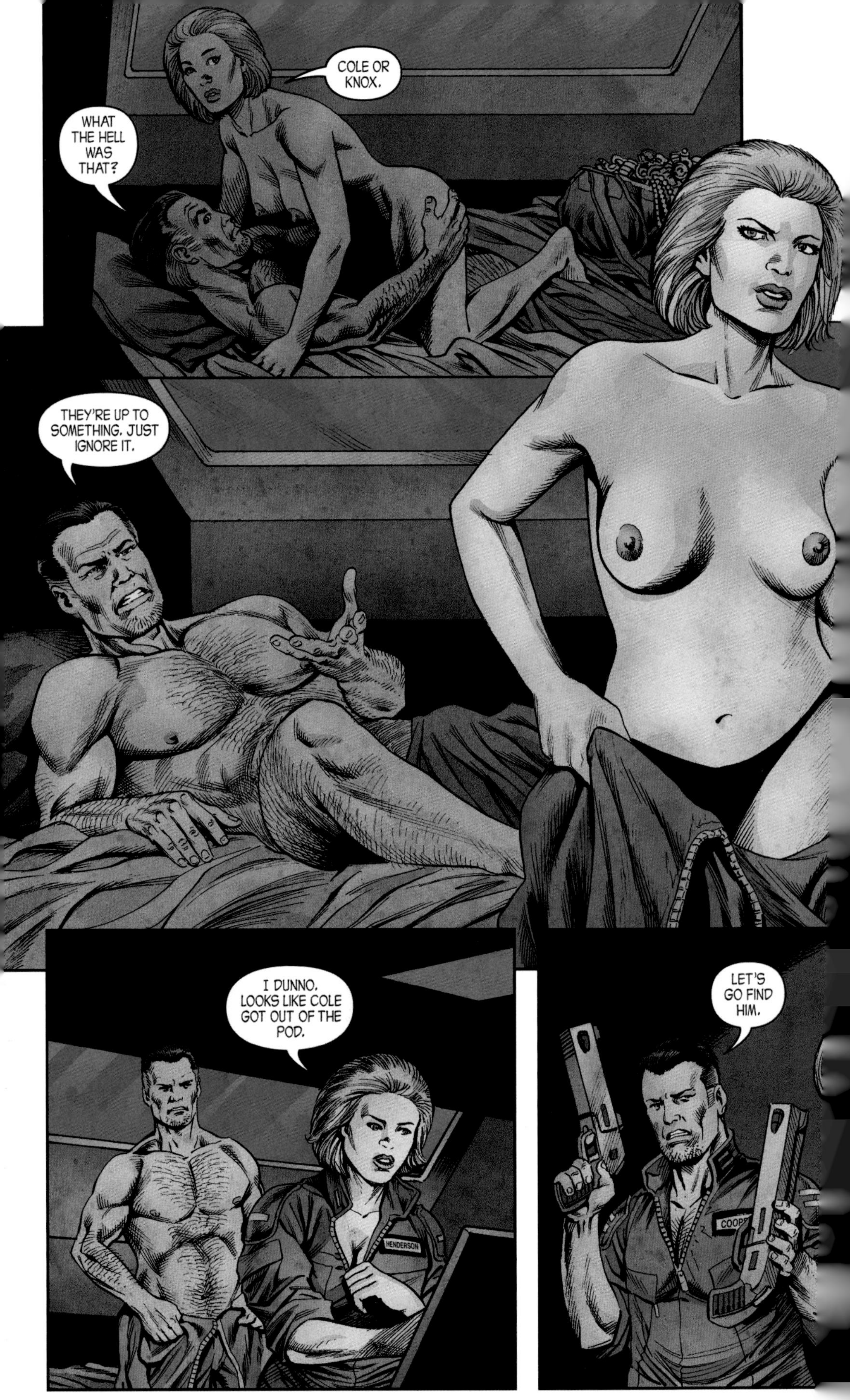
COLE OR KNOX.
WHAT THE HELL WAS THAT?
THEY'RE UP TO SOMETHING. JUST IGNORE IT.
I DUNNO. LOOKS LIKE COLE GOT OUT OF THE POD.
HENDERSON
LET'S GO FIND HIM.

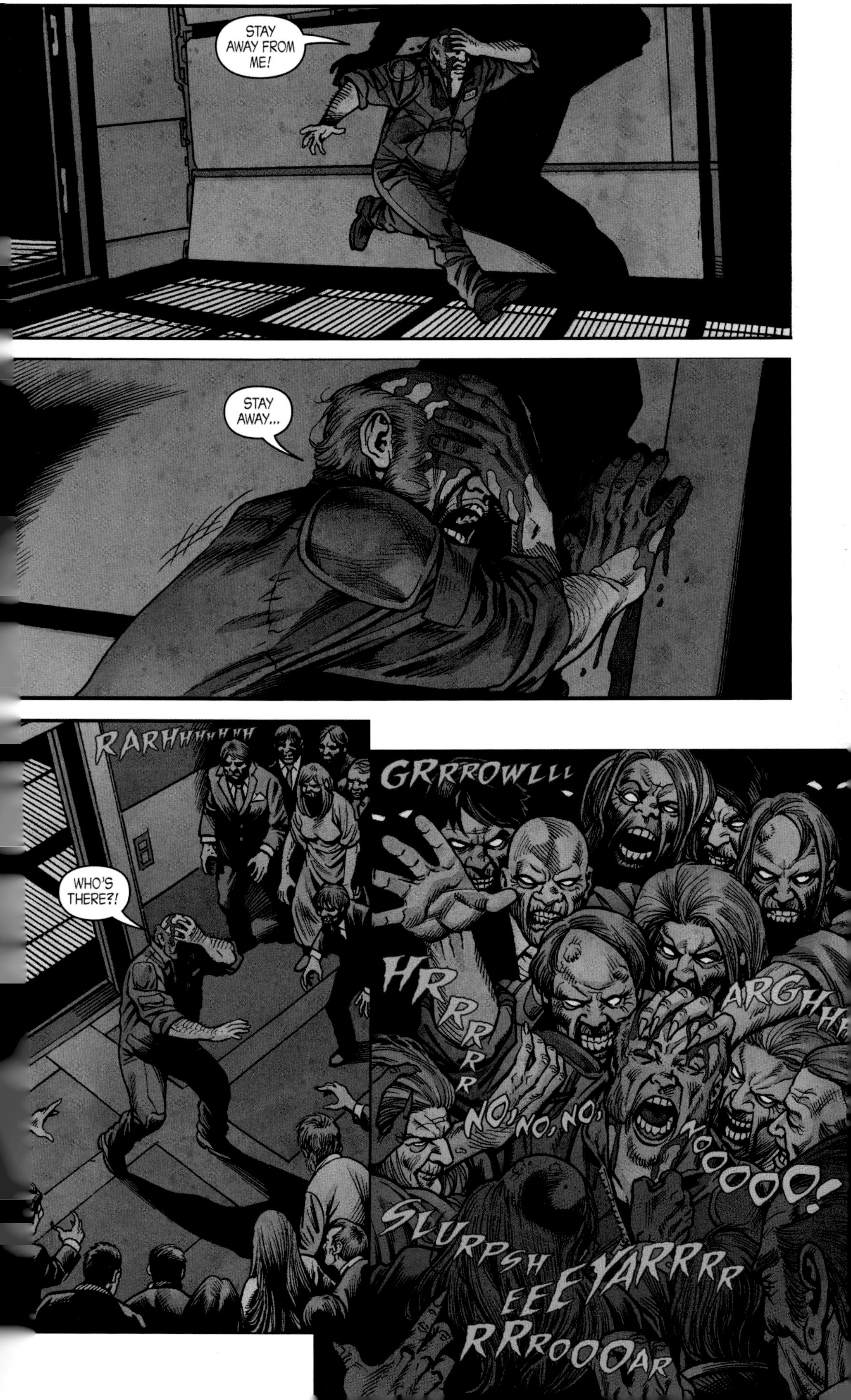

STAY AWAY FROM ME!
STAY AWAY...
RARHHHHHH
WHO'S THERE?!
GRRROWLLL
HRRRRR
NO, NO, NO, NOOOOO!
ARGHH
SLURPSH
EEEYARRRRR
RRROOOOAR

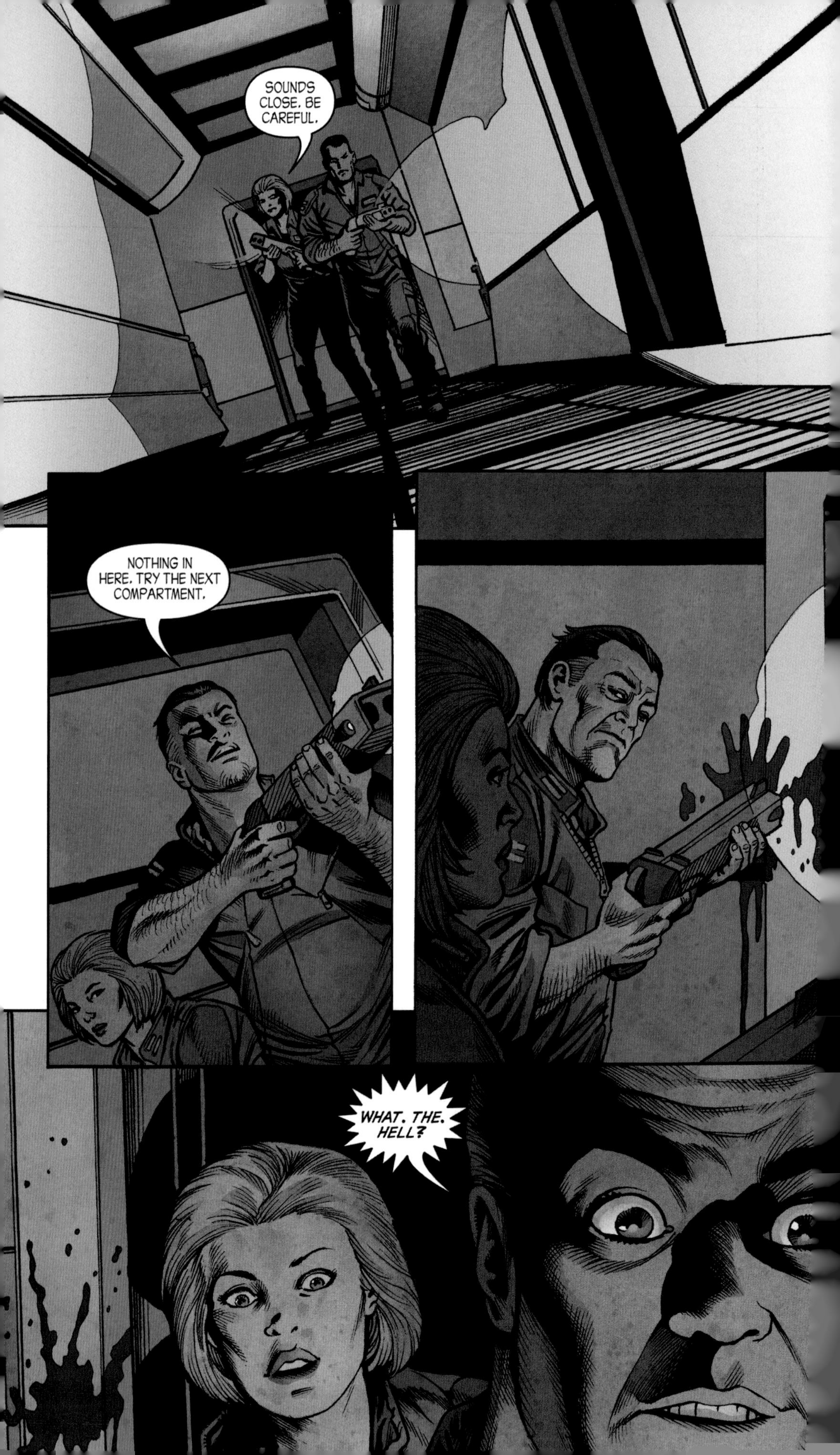
SOUNDS CLOSE. BE CAREFUL.
NOTHING IN HERE. TRY THE NEXT COMPARTMENT.
WHAT. THE. HELL?

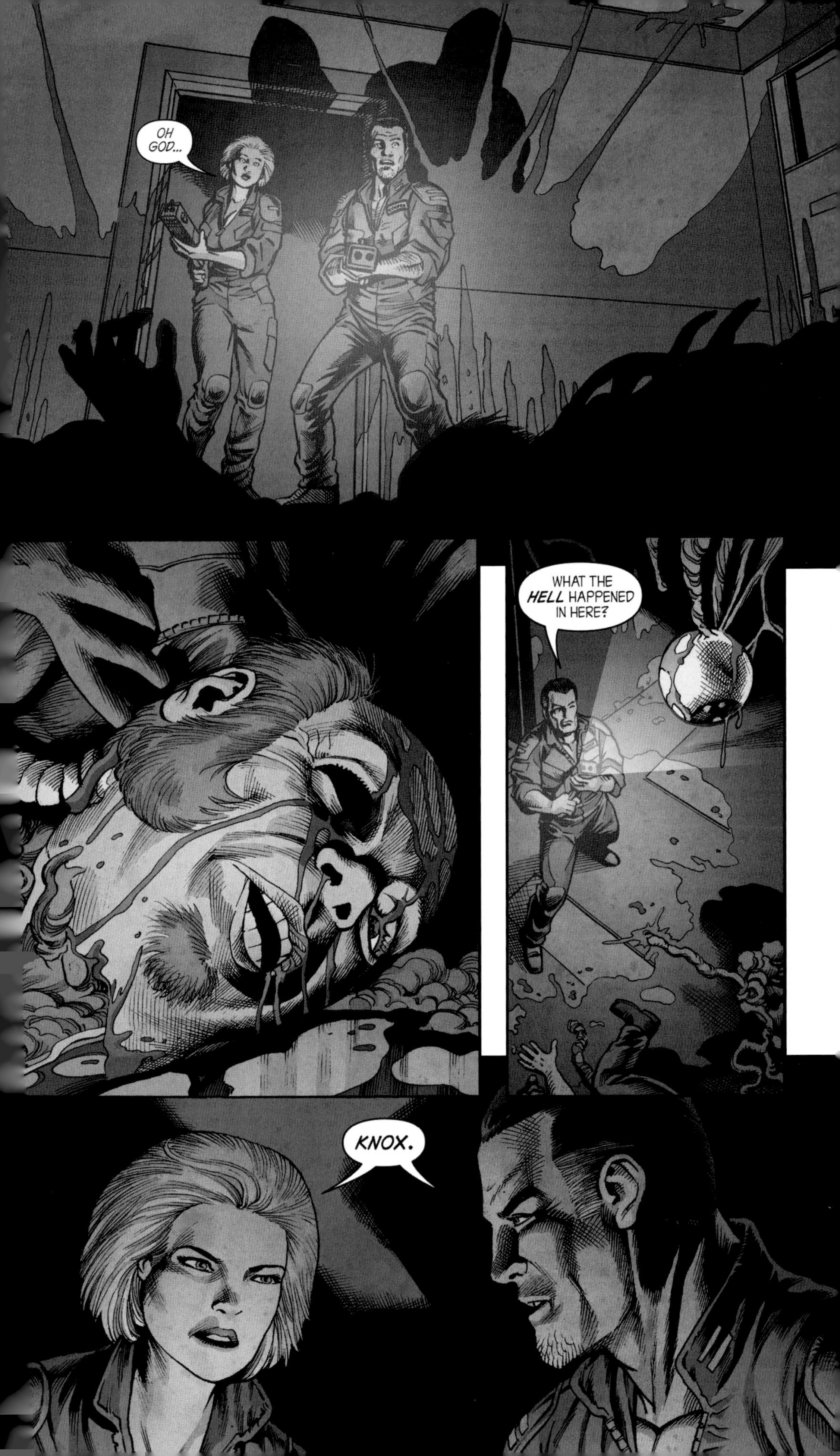
OH GOD...
WHAT THE HELL HAPPENED IN HERE?
KNOX.

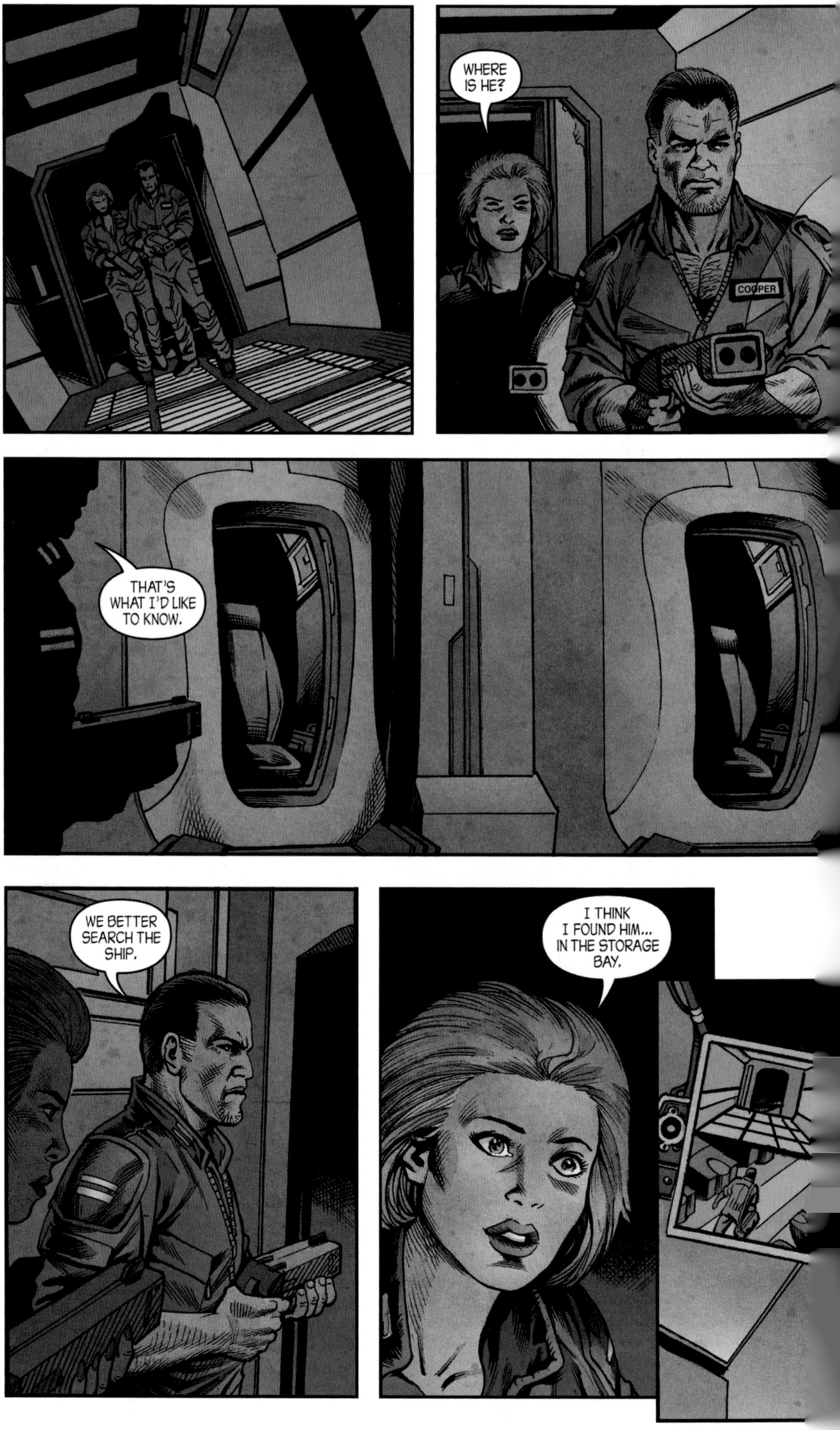
WHERE IS HE?
COOPER
THAT'S WHAT I'D LIKE TO KNOW.
WE BETTER SEARCH THE SHIP.
I THINK I FOUND HIM... IN THE STORAGE BAY.

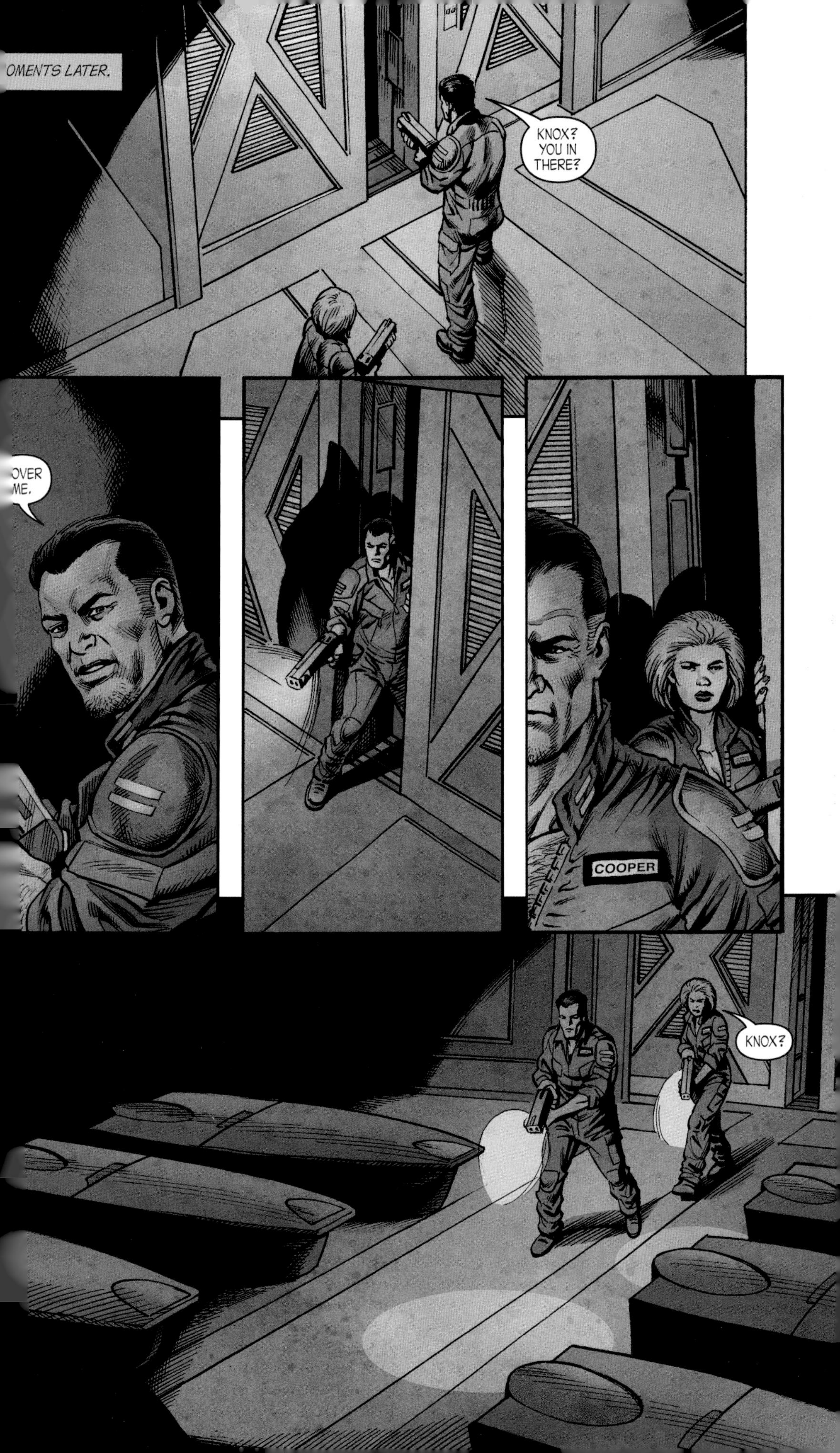
OMENTS LATER.
KNOX? YOU IN THERE?
OVER ME.
COOPER
KNOX?

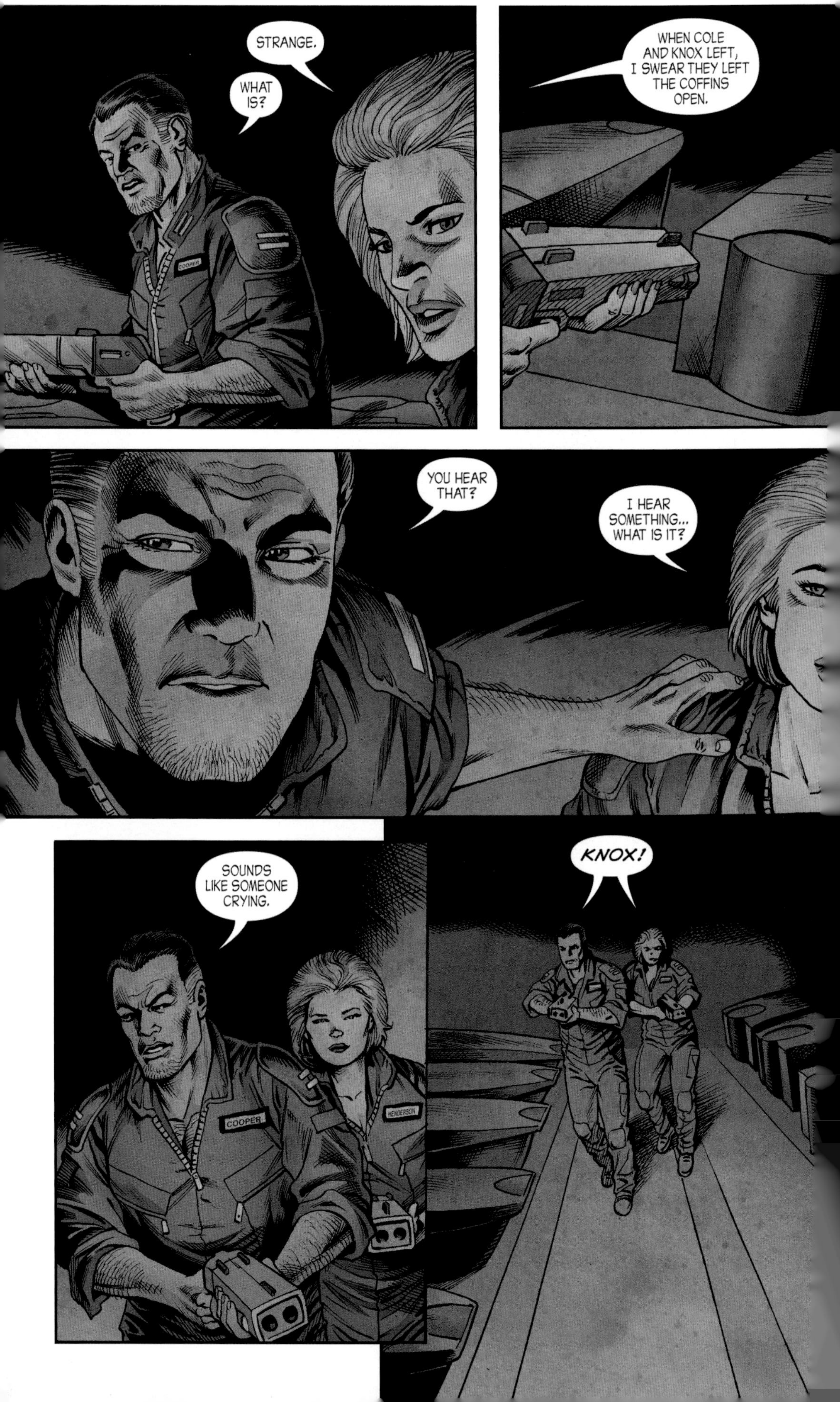
STRANGE.
WHAT IS?
WHEN COLE AND KNOX LEFT, I SWEAR THEY LEFT THE COFFINS OPEN.
COOPER
YOU HEAR THAT?
I HEAR SOMETHING... WHAT IS IT?
SOUNDS LIKE SOMEONE CRYING.
COOPER
HENDERSON
KNOX!

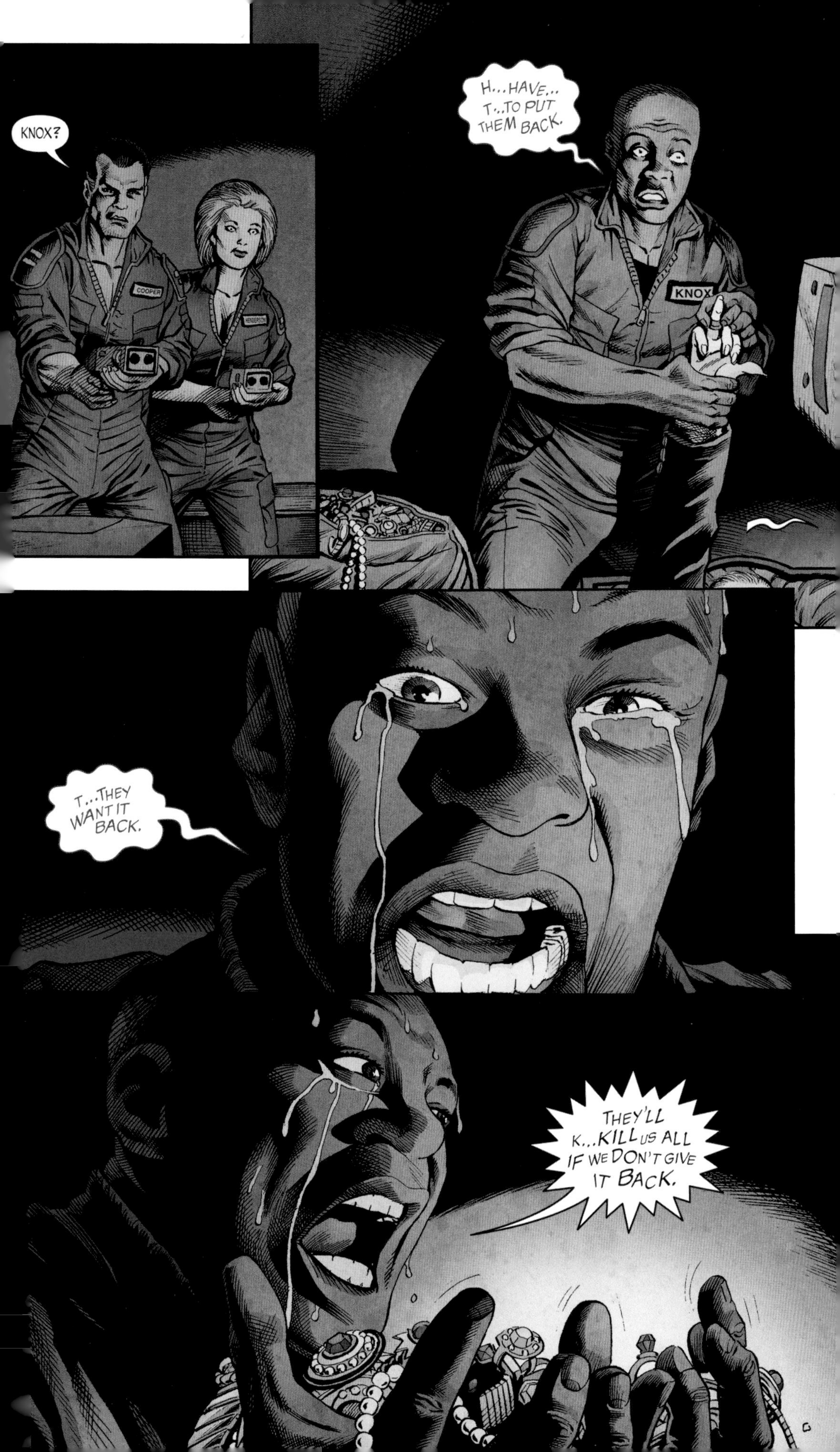
KNOX?
COOPER
HENDERSON
H...HAVE... T-..TO PUT THEM BACK.
KNOX
T...THEY WANT IT BACK.
THEY'LL K...KILL US ALL IF WE DON'T GIVE IT BACK.

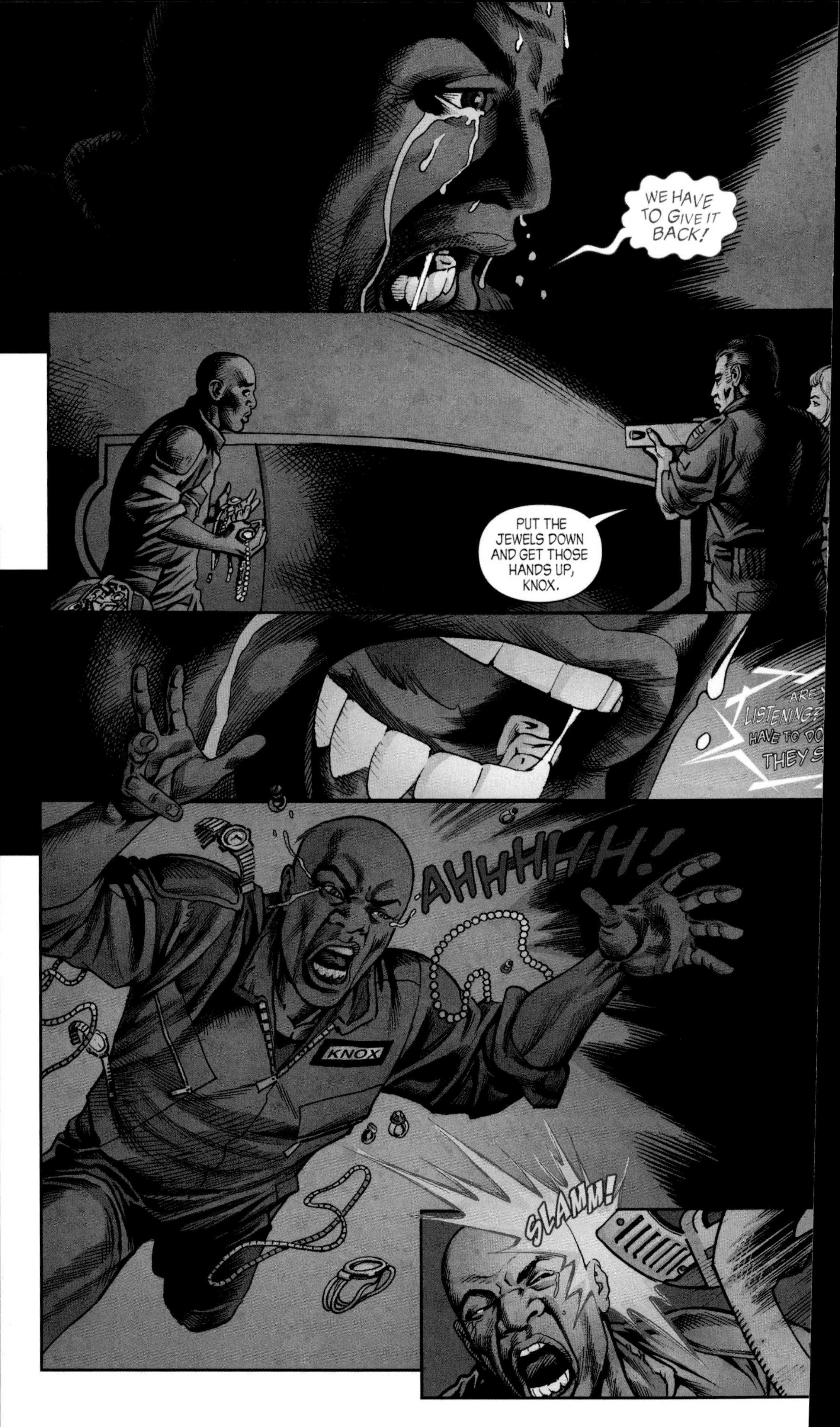
WE HAVE TO GIVE IT BACK!
PUT THE JEWELS DOWN AND GET THOSE HANDS UP, KNOX.
LISTENING?
AHHHHHH!
KNOX
SLAMM!

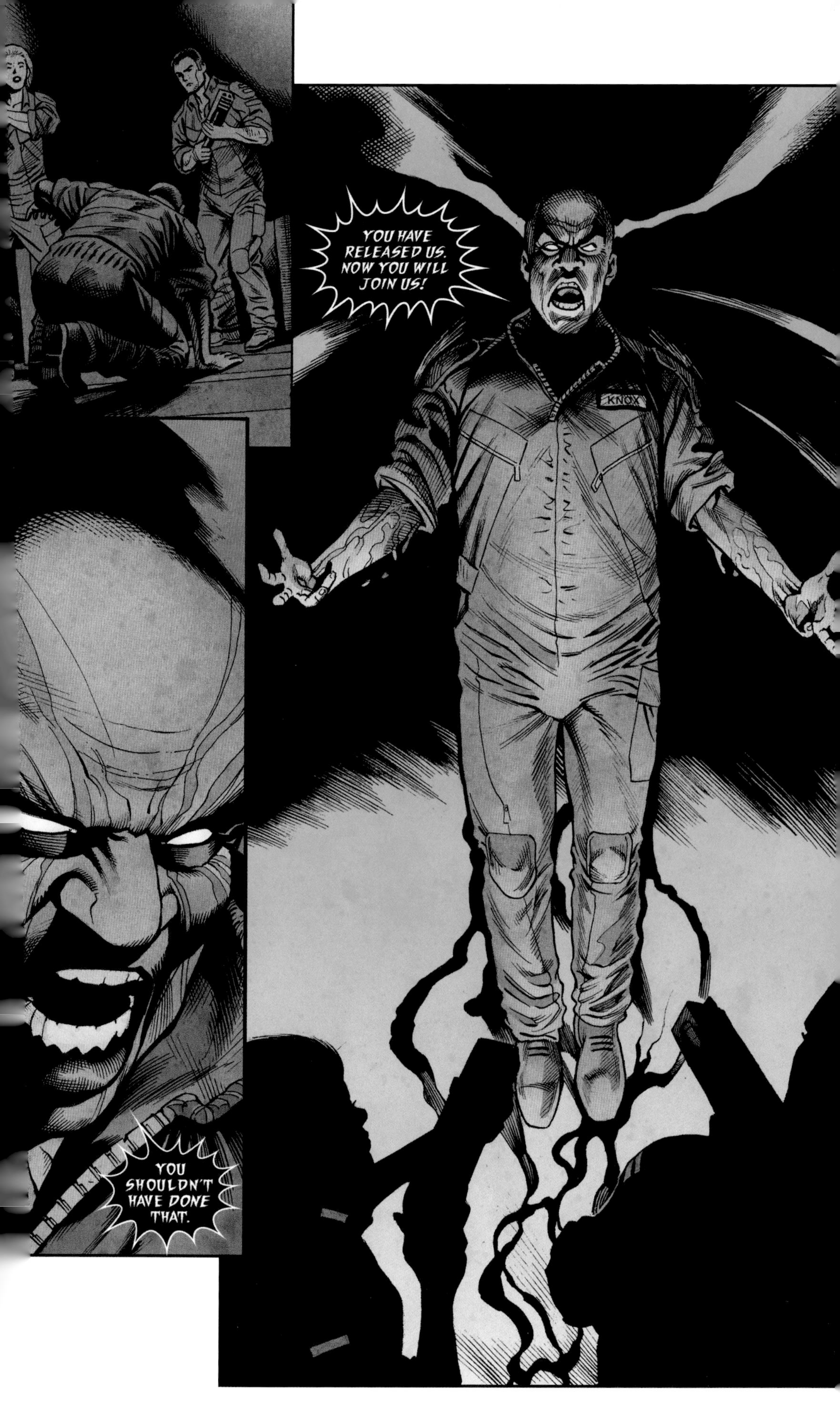
YOU HAVE RELEASED US. NOW YOU WILL JOIN US!
YOU SHOULDN'T HAVE DONE THAT.

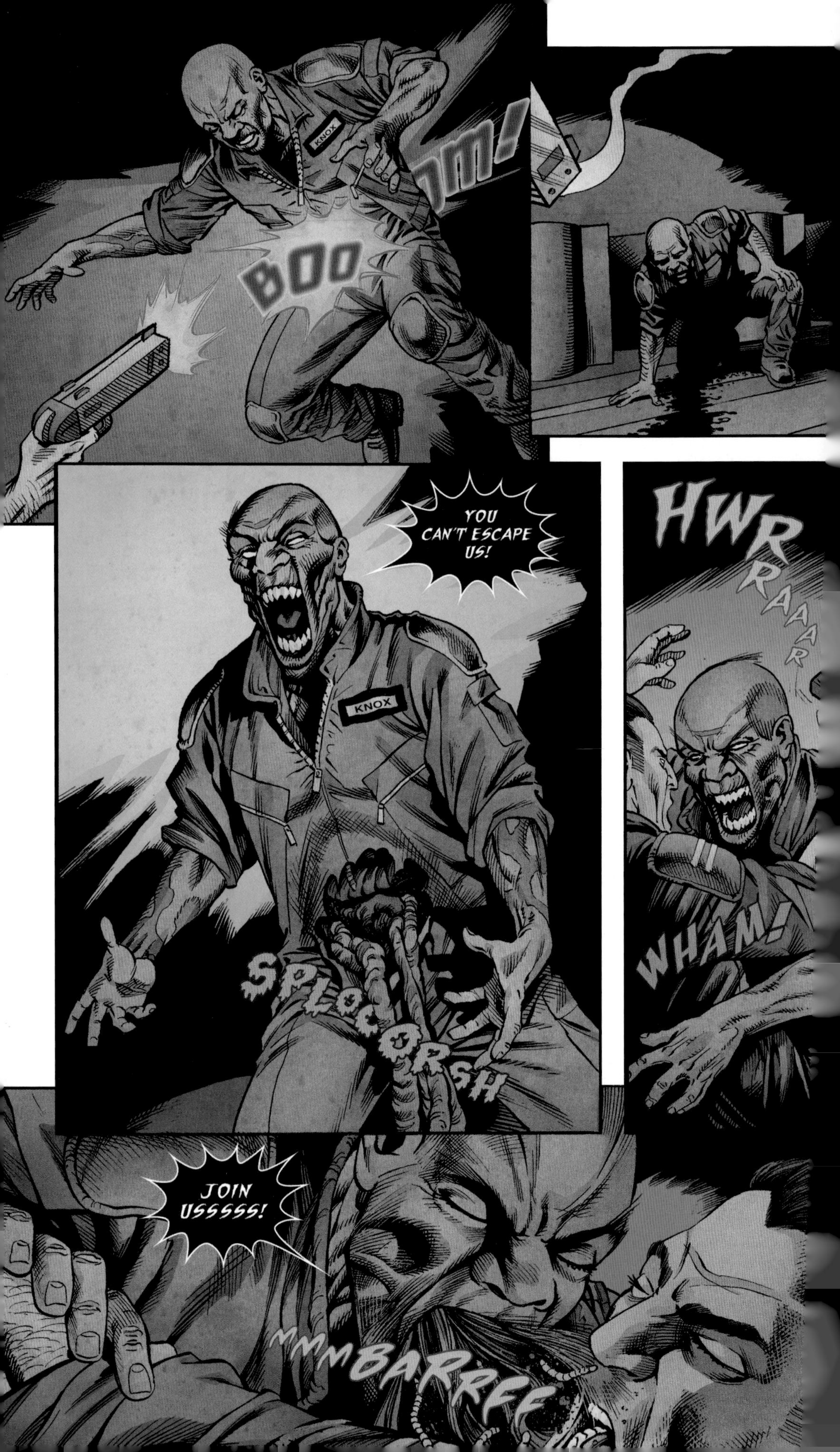
KNOX
BOOOM!
YOU CAN'T ESCAPE US!
KNOX
SPLOCCORSH
HWRRAAAAR
WHAM!
JOIN USSSSS!
MMMBARRFF

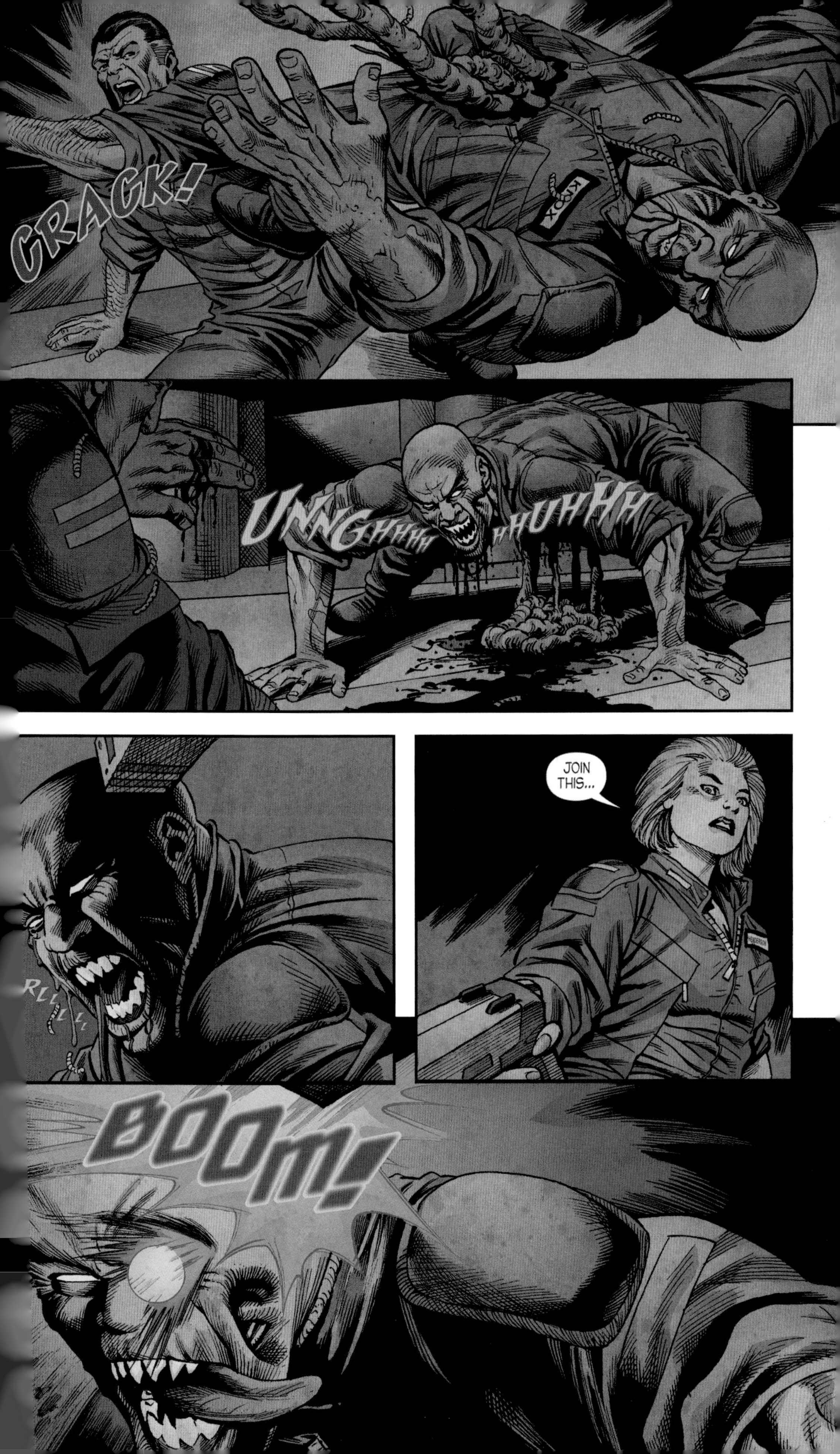
CRACK!
KNOX
UNNGHHHH HHUHHHH
RLLLLL
JOIN THIS...
BOOM!

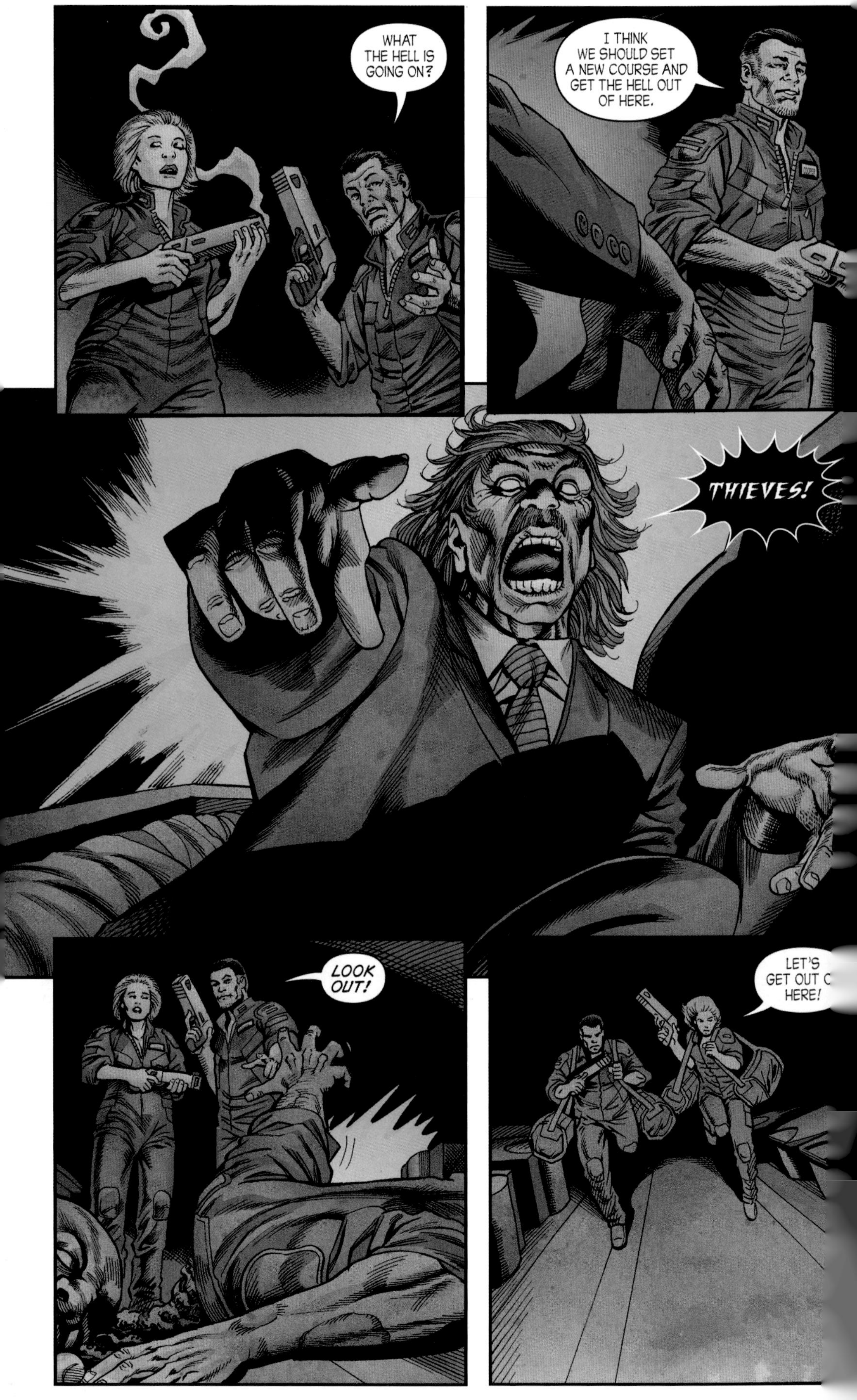
WHAT THE HELL IS GOING ON?
I THINK WE SHOULD SET A NEW COURSE AND GET THE HELL OUT OF HERE.
THIEVES!
LOOK OUT!
LET'S GET OUT O HERE!

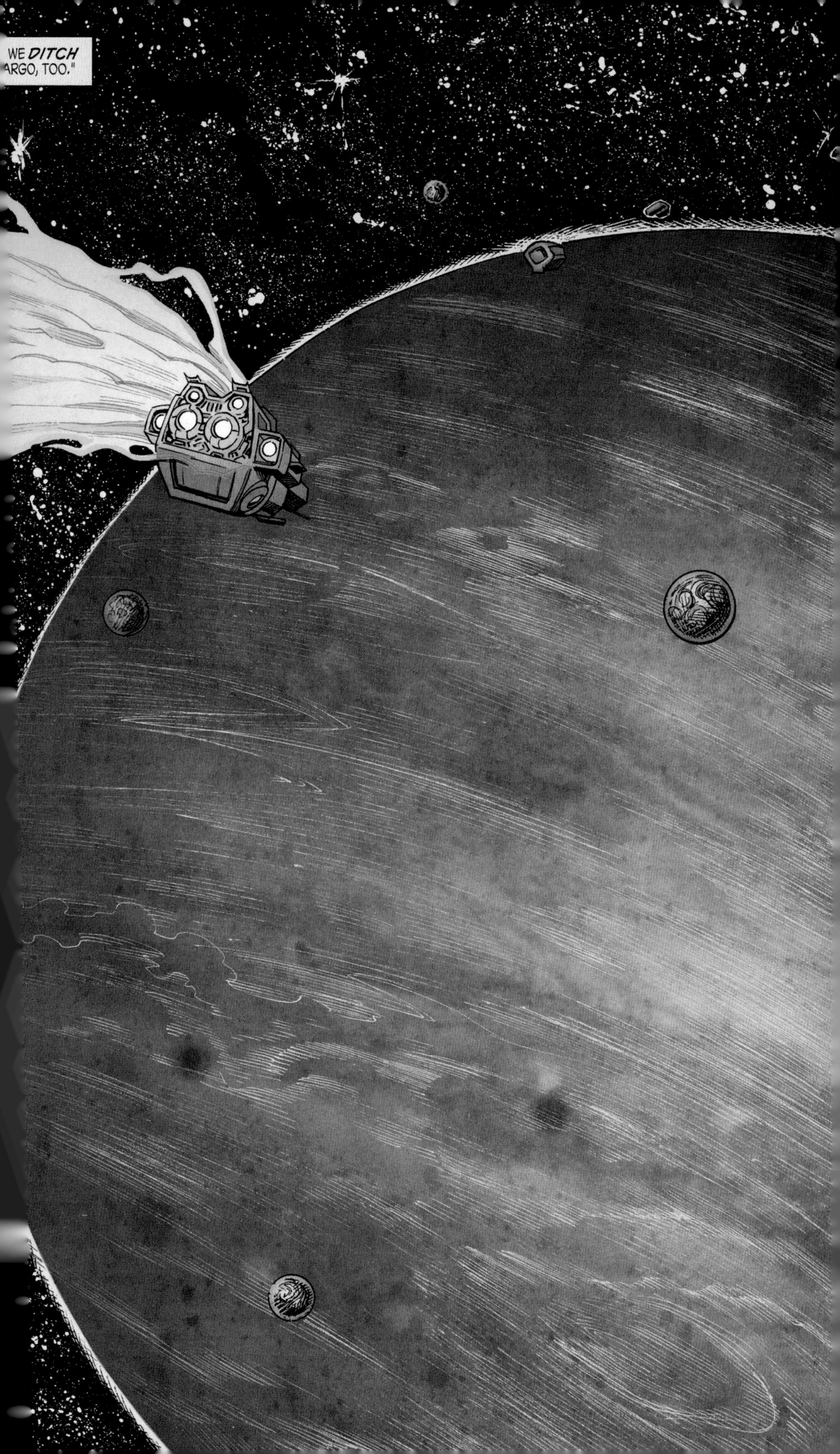
WE DITCH
ARGO, TOO."

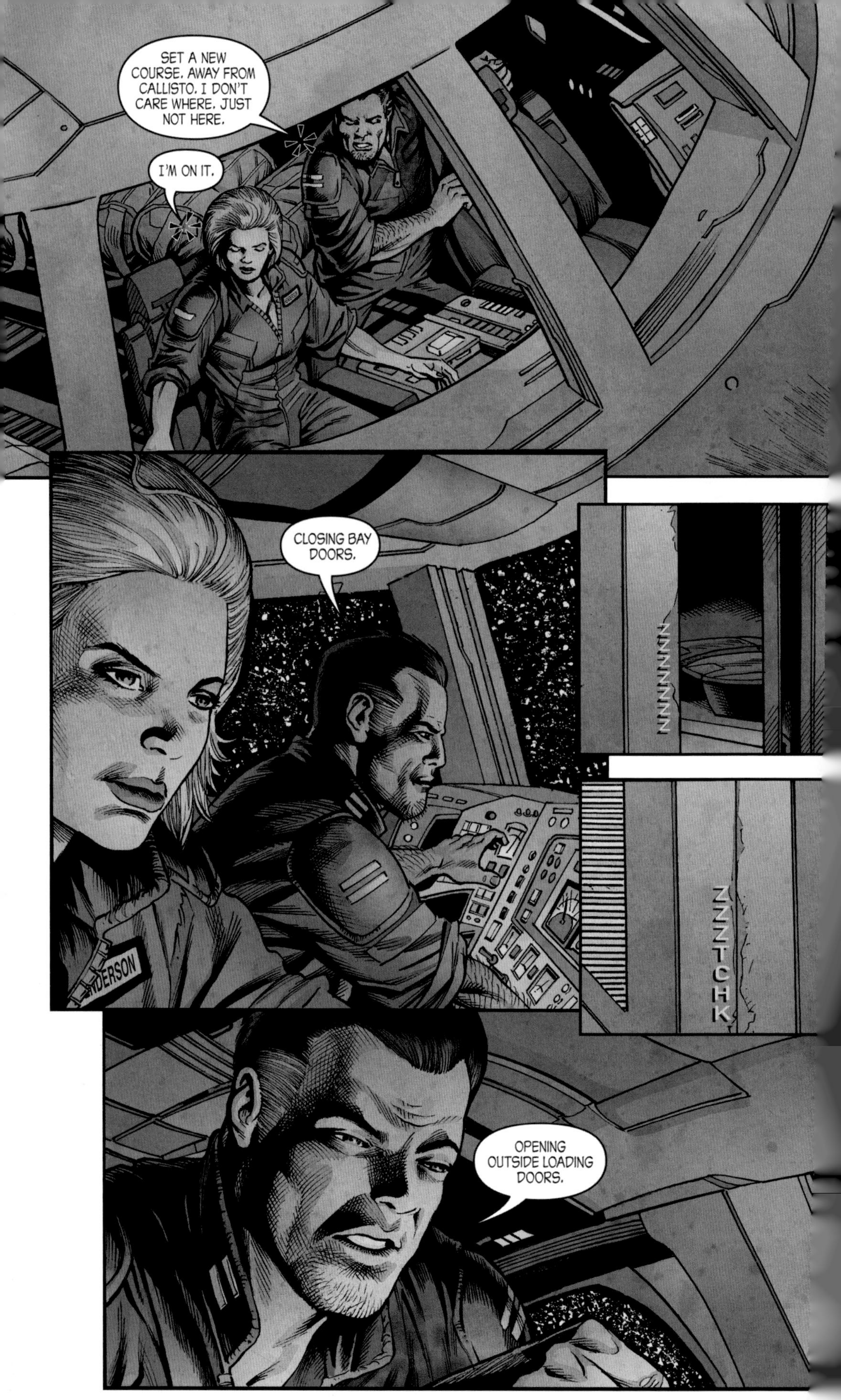

SET A NEW COURSE. AWAY FROM CALLISTO. I DON'T CARE WHERE. JUST NOT HERE.
I'M ON IT.
CLOSING BAY DOORS.
NNNNNNN
ZZZTCHK
OPENING OUTSIDE LOADING DOORS.

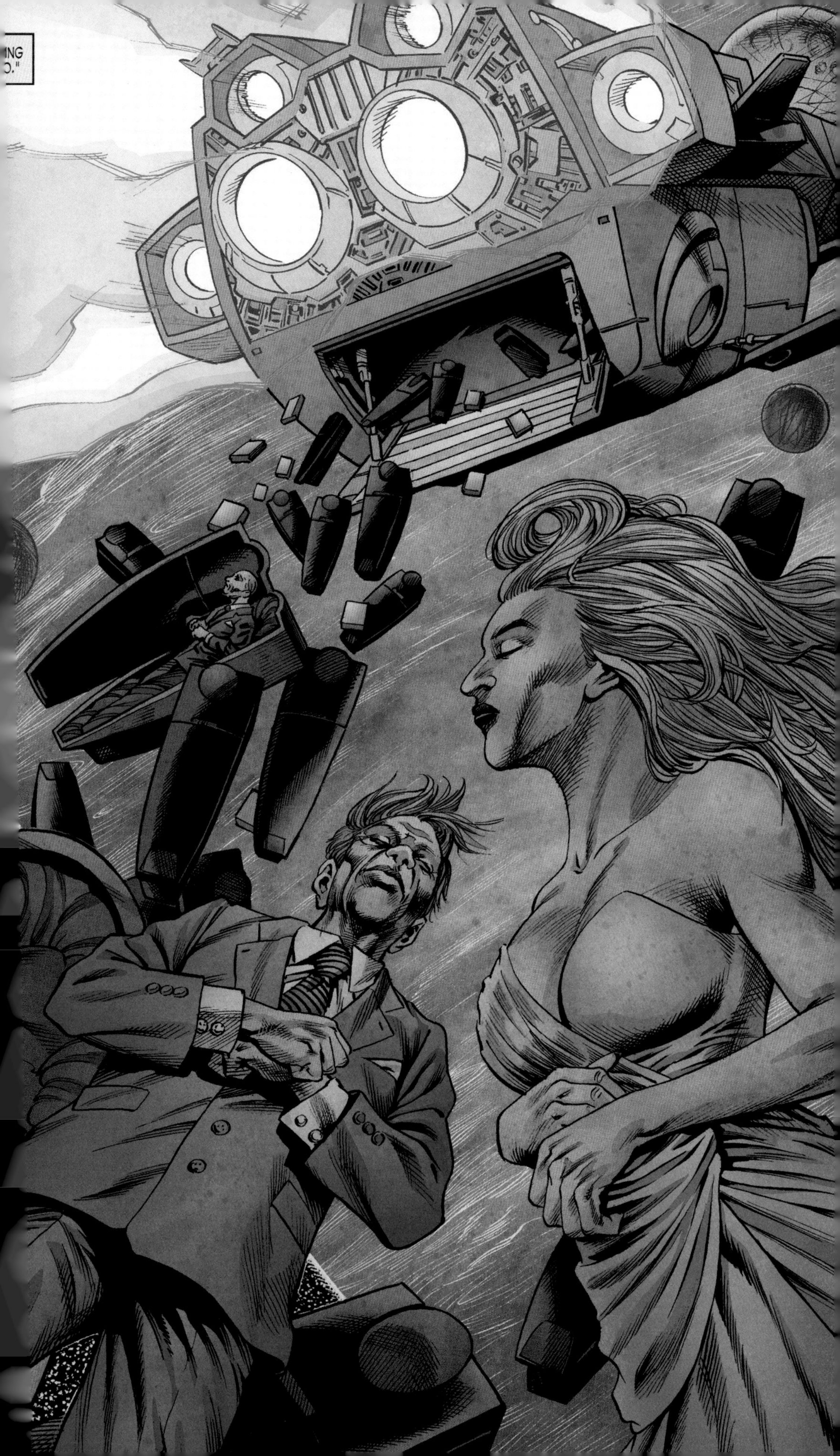

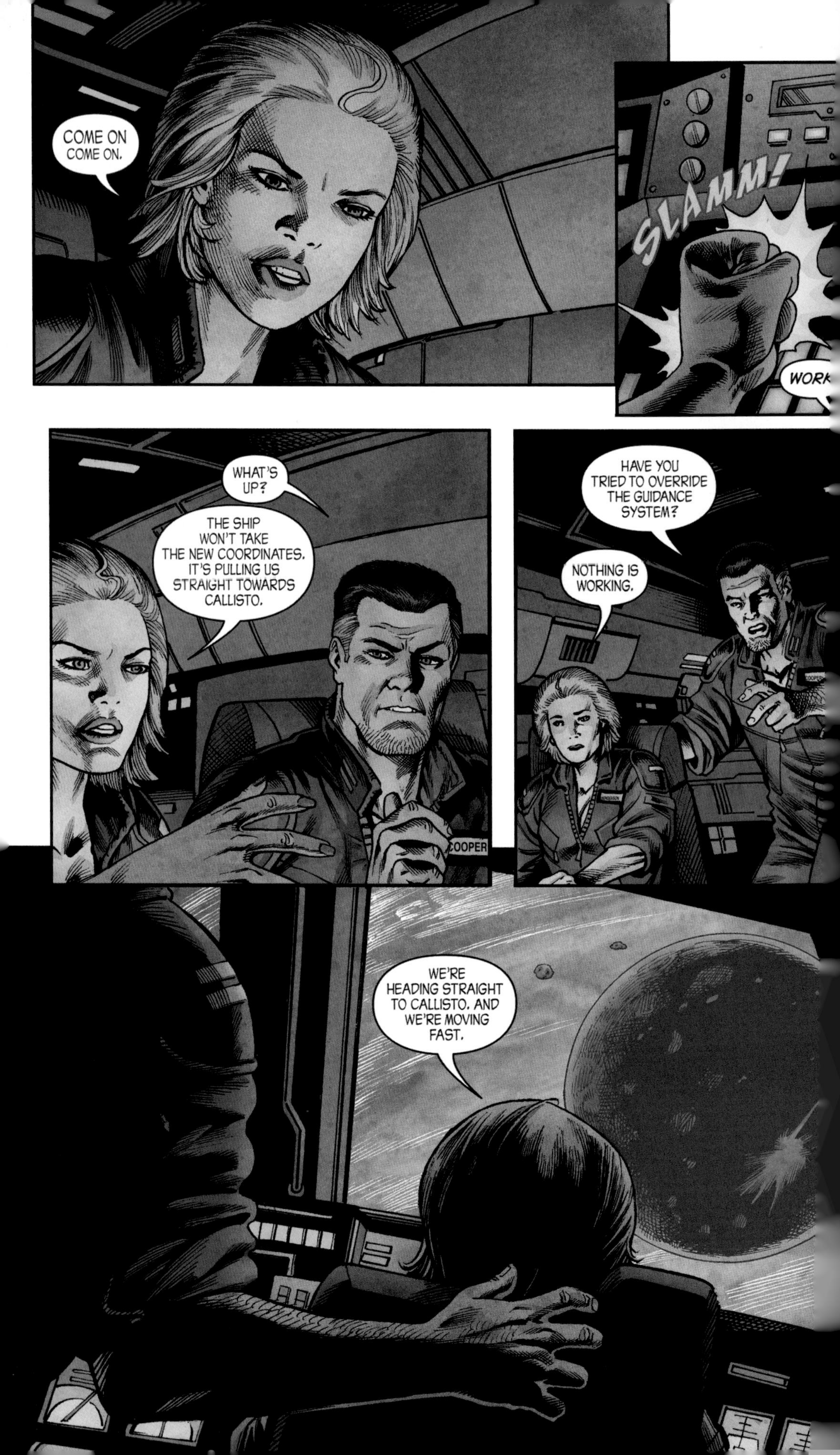
COME ON
COME ON.
SLAMM!
WORK
WHAT'S UP?
THE SHIP WON'T TAKE THE NEW COORDINATES. IT'S PULLING US STRAIGHT TOWARDS CALLISTO.
COOPER
HAVE YOU TRIED TO OVERRIDE THE GUIDANCE SYSTEM?
NOTHING IS WORKING.
WE'RE HEADING STRAIGHT TO CALLISTO. AND WE'RE MOVING FAST.

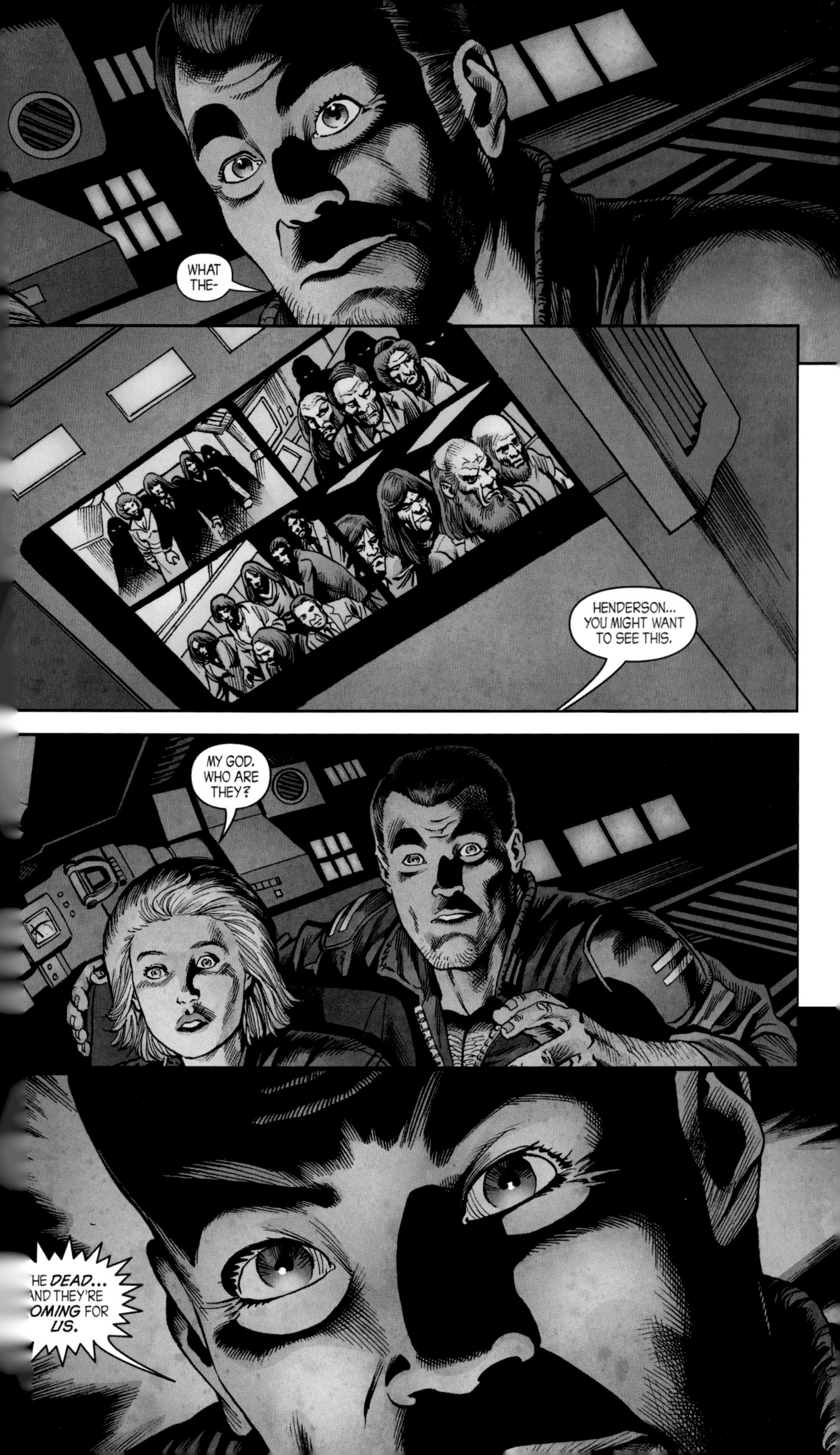
WHAT THE-
HENDERSON... YOU MIGHT WANT TO SEE THIS.
MY GOD. WHO ARE THEY?
HE *DEAD*... AND THEY'RE *OMING* FOR *US.*

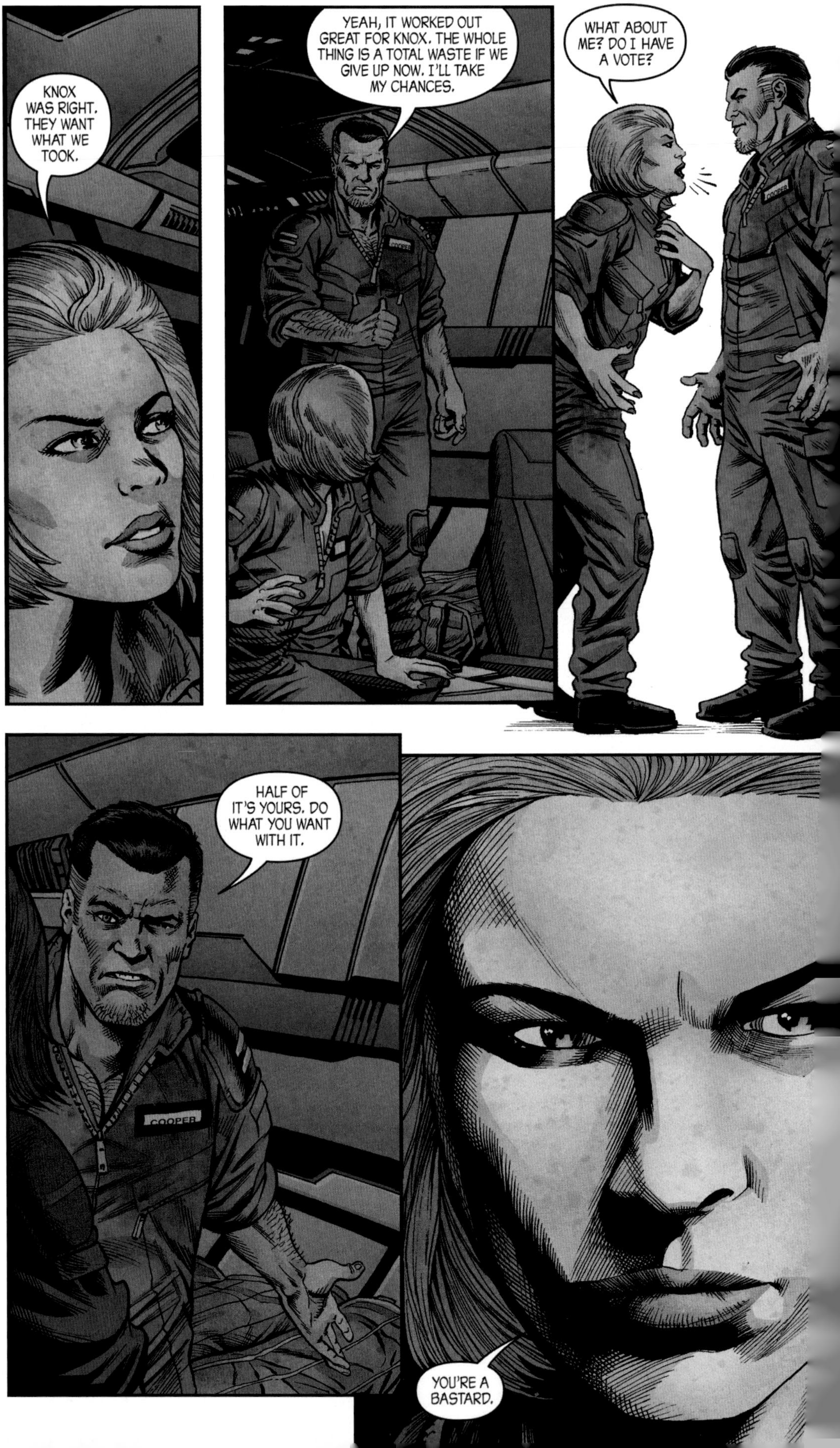
KNOX WAS RIGHT. THEY WANT WHAT WE TOOK.
YEAH, IT WORKED OUT GREAT FOR KNOX. THE WHOLE THING IS A TOTAL WASTE IF WE GIVE UP NOW. I'LL TAKE MY CHANCES.
WHAT ABOUT ME? DO I HAVE A VOTE?
HALF OF IT'S YOURS. DO WHAT YOU WANT WITH IT.
YOU'RE A BASTARD.

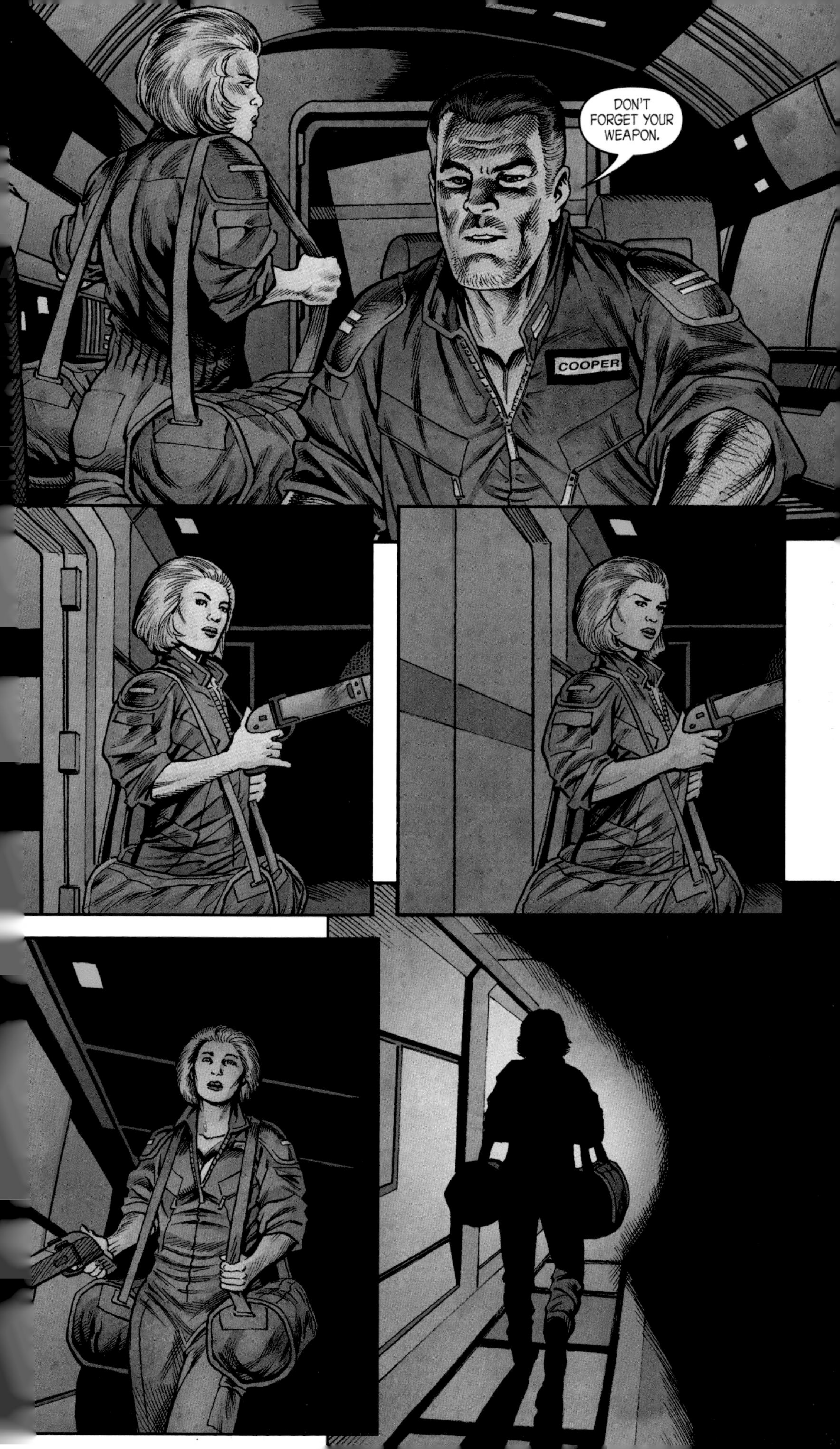
DON'T FORGET YOUR WEAPON.
COOPER

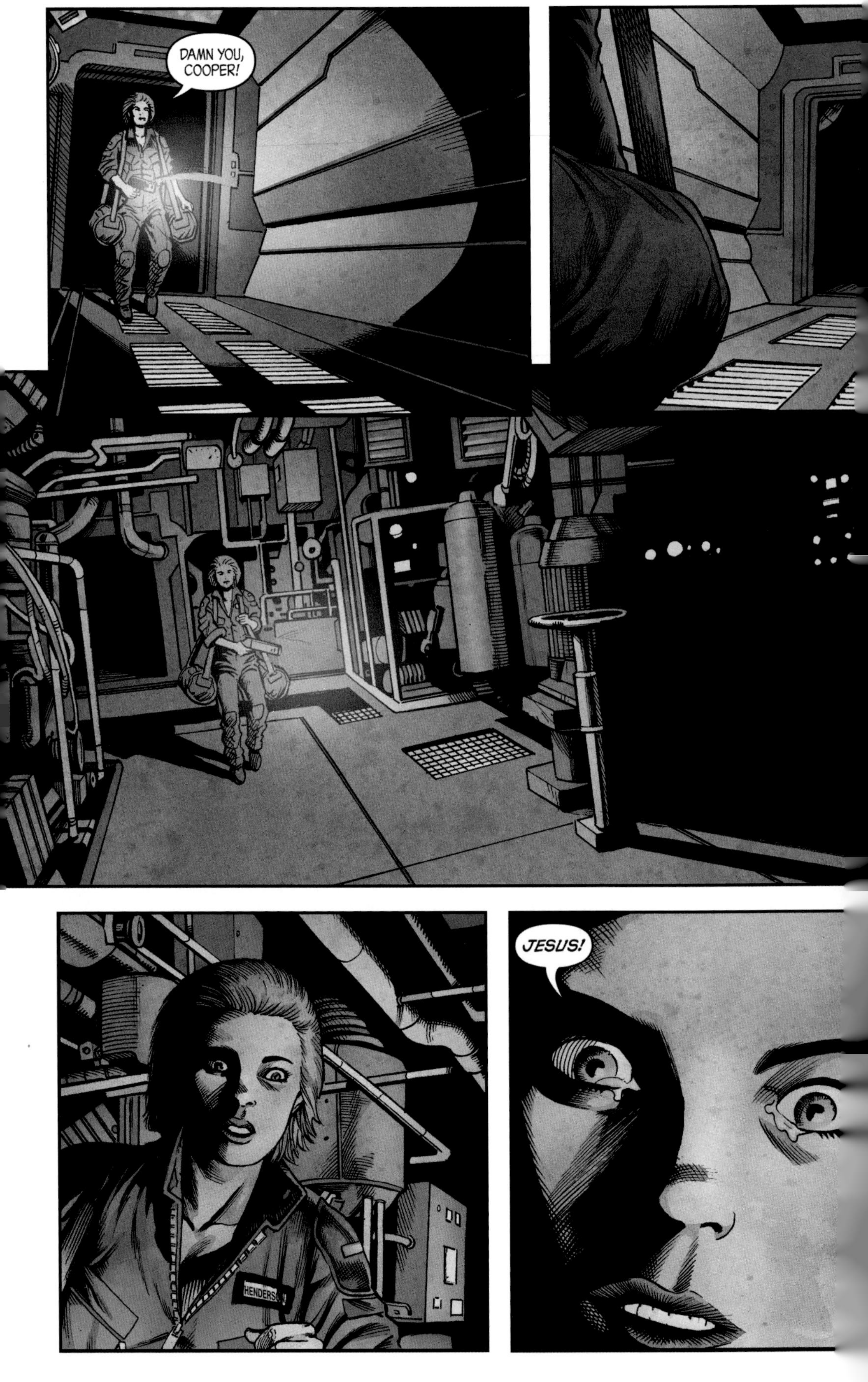
DAMN YOU, COOPER!
HENDERSON
JESUS!

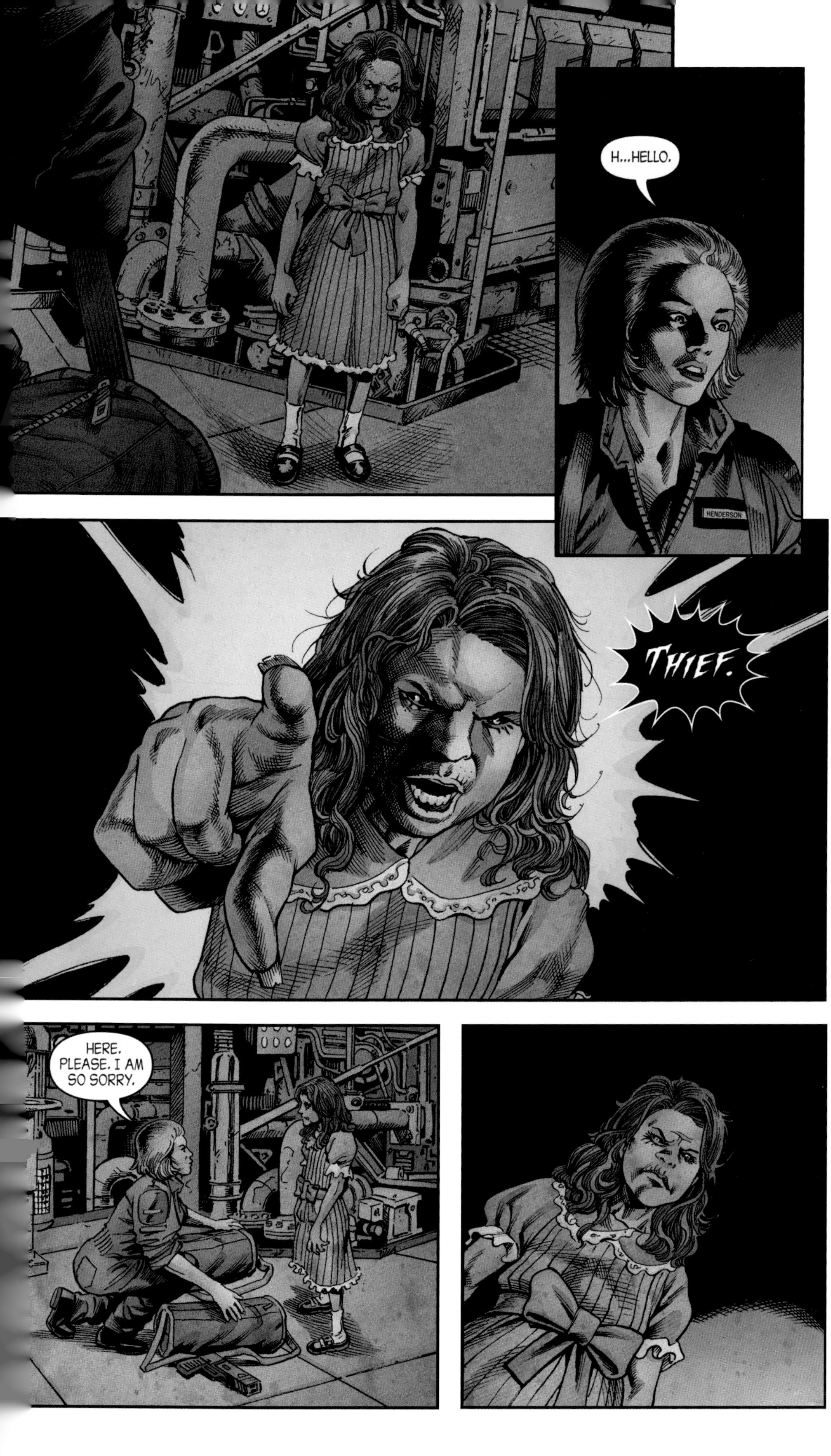
H...HELLO.
HENDERSON
THIEF.
HERE. PLEASE. I AM SO SORRY.

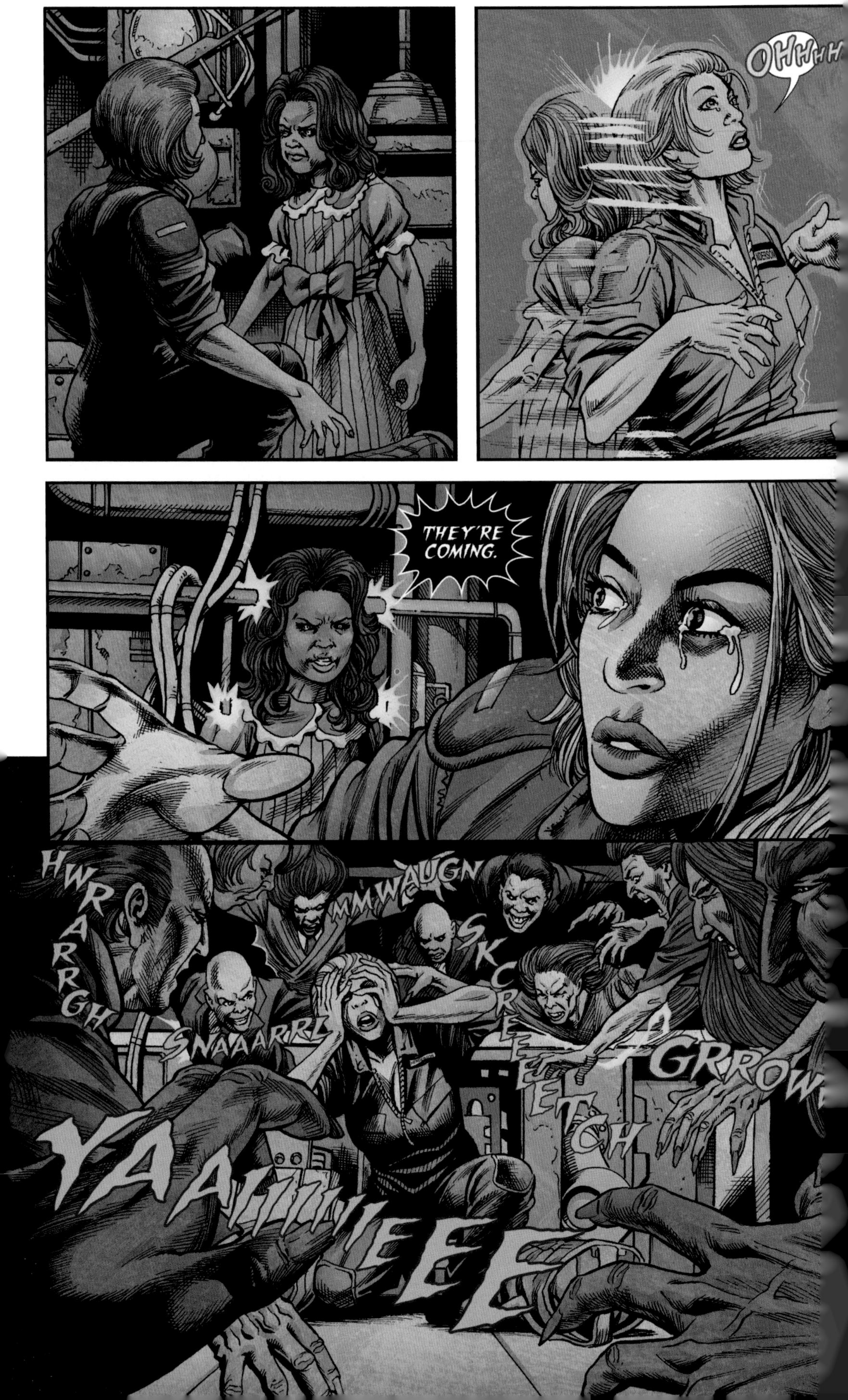

OHHHHH
THEY'RE COMING.
HWRARRGH
MMWAUGN
SKCREEETCH
SNAAARRL
GRROW
YAAIIIIIEEE

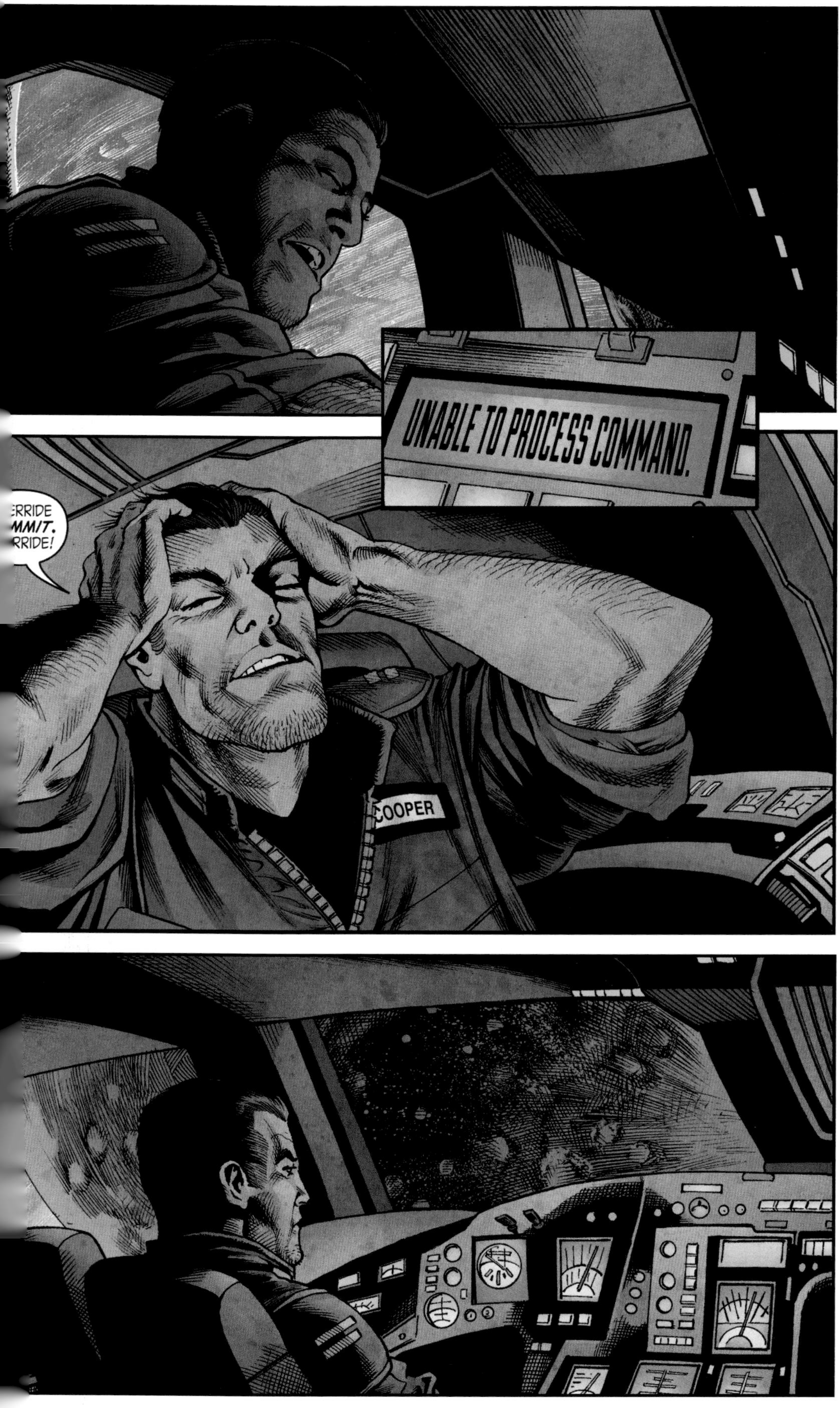
UNABLE TO PROCESS COMMAND.
ERRIDE
MMIT.
RRIDE!
COOPER

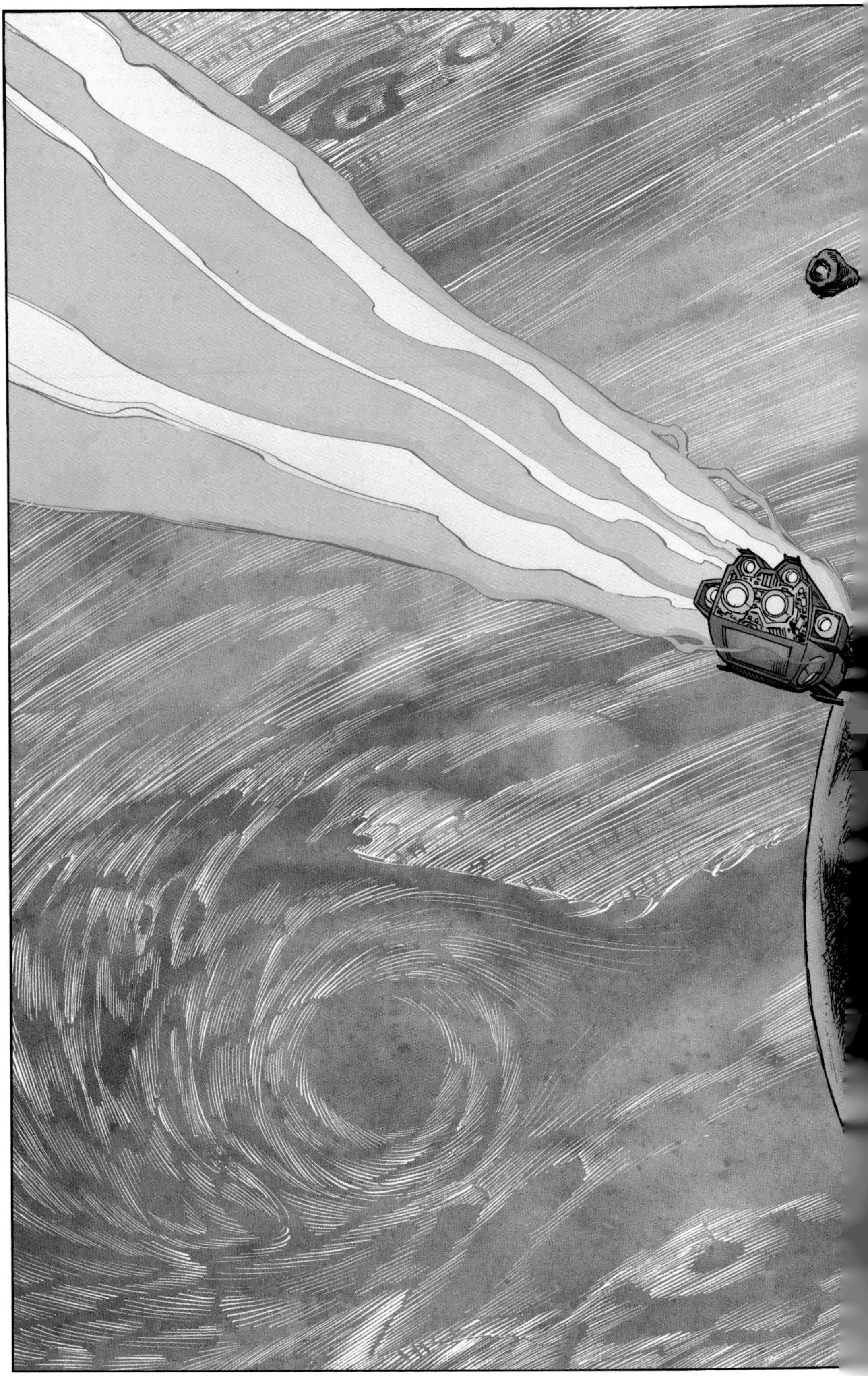

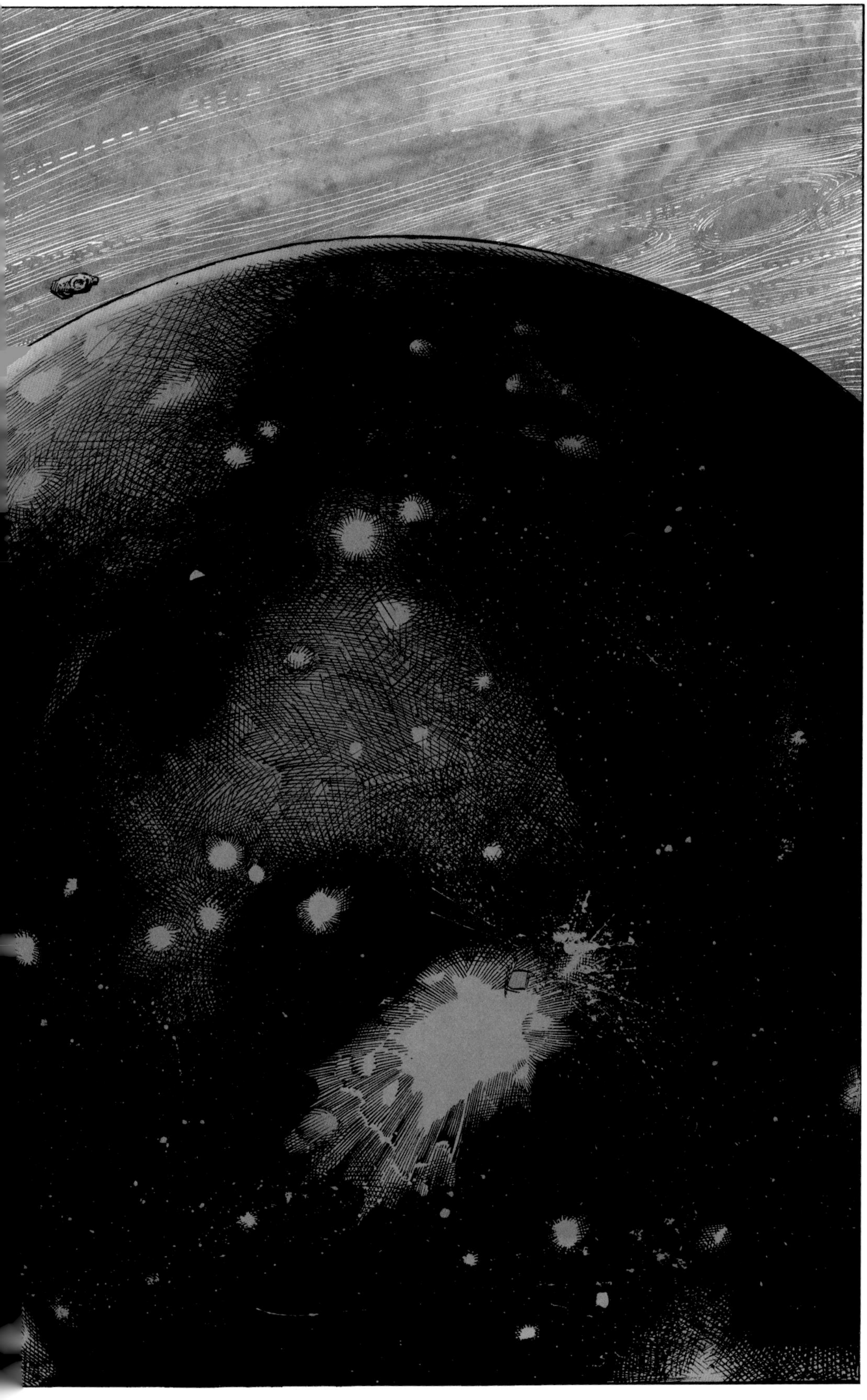

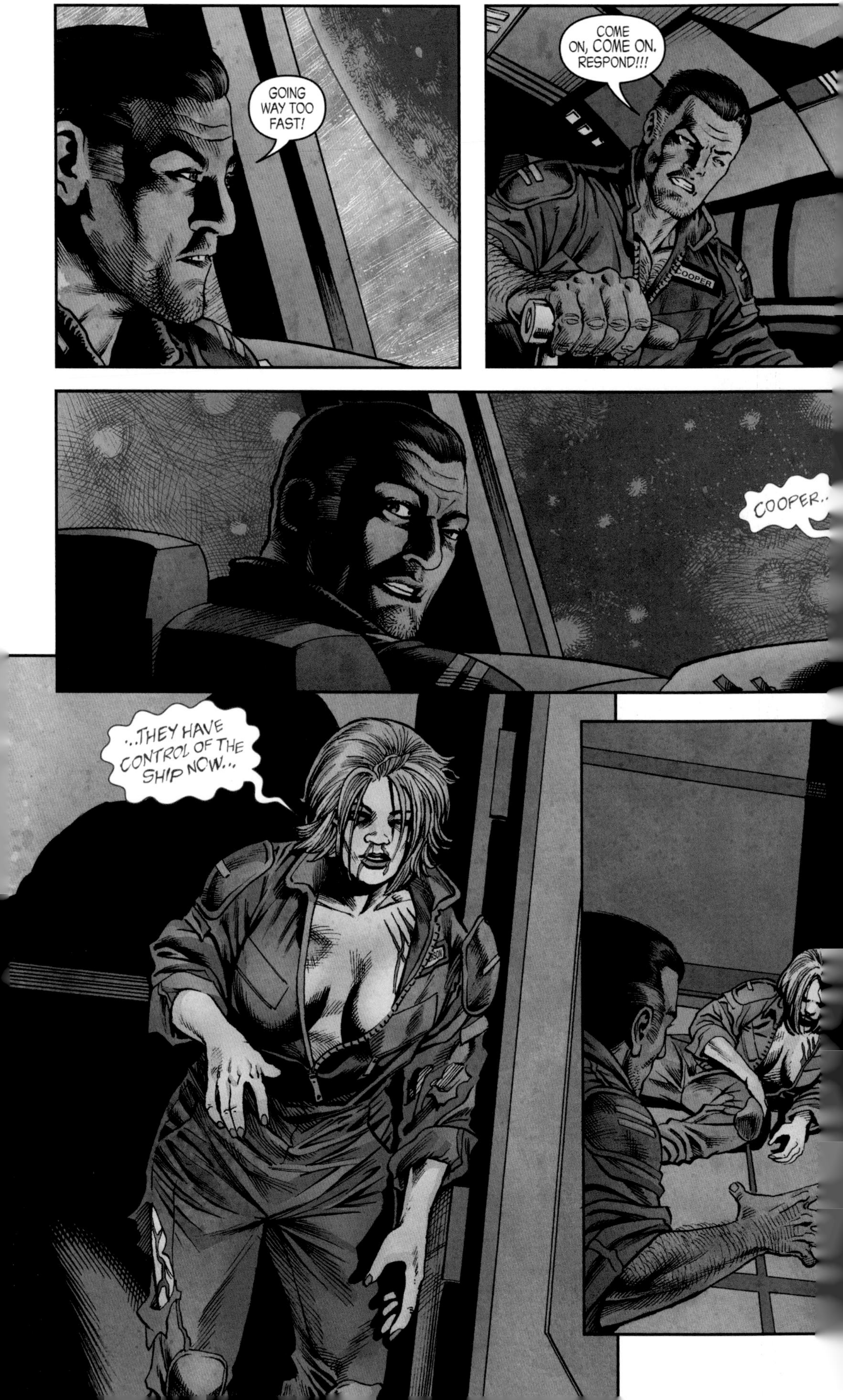
GOING WAY TOO FAST!
COME ON, COME ON. RESPOND!!!
COOPER
COOPER...
...THEY HAVE CONTROL OF THE SHIP NOW...

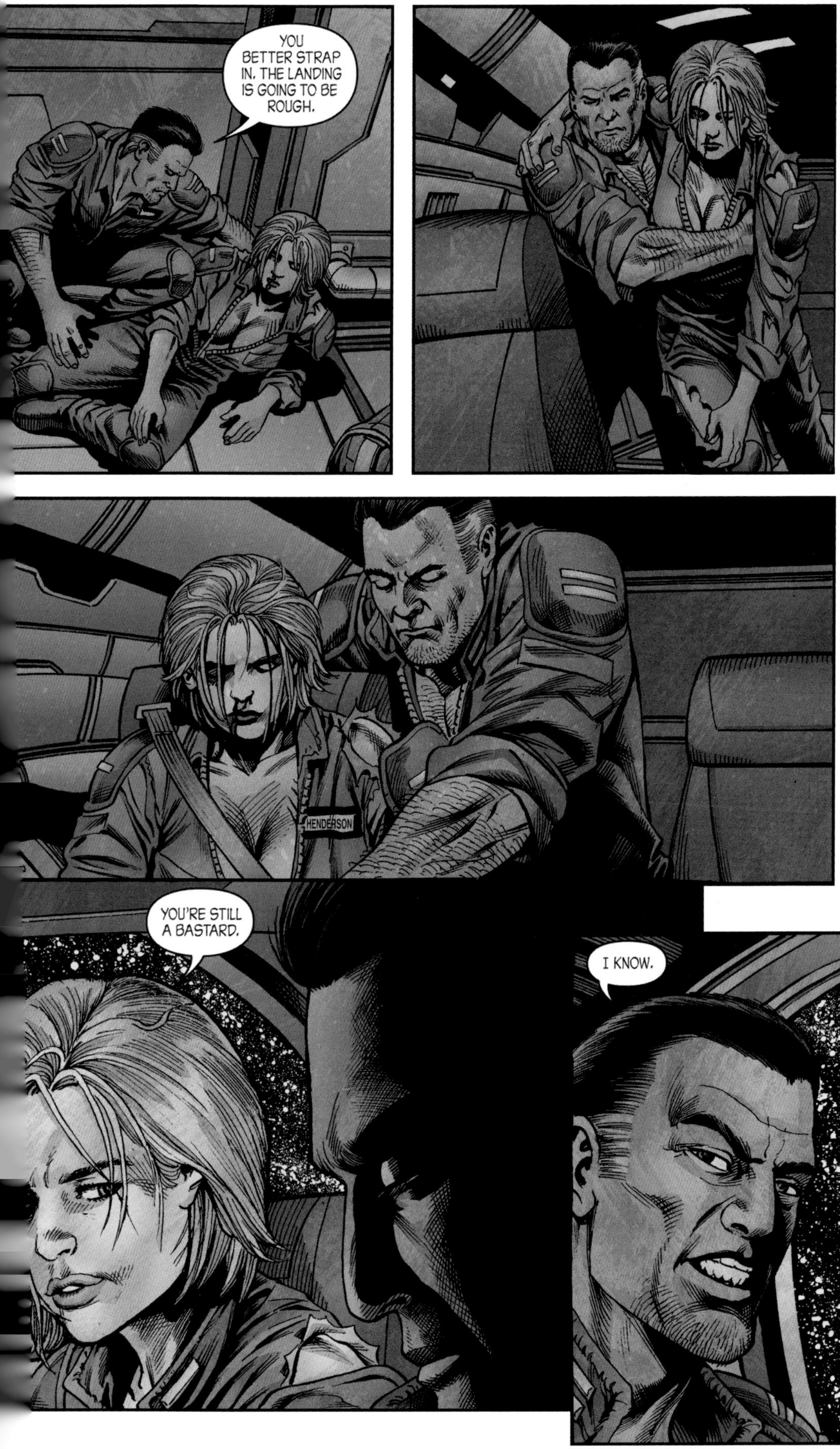
YOU BETTER STRAP IN. THE LANDING IS GOING TO BE ROUGH.
HENDERSON
YOU'RE STILL A BASTARD.
I KNOW.

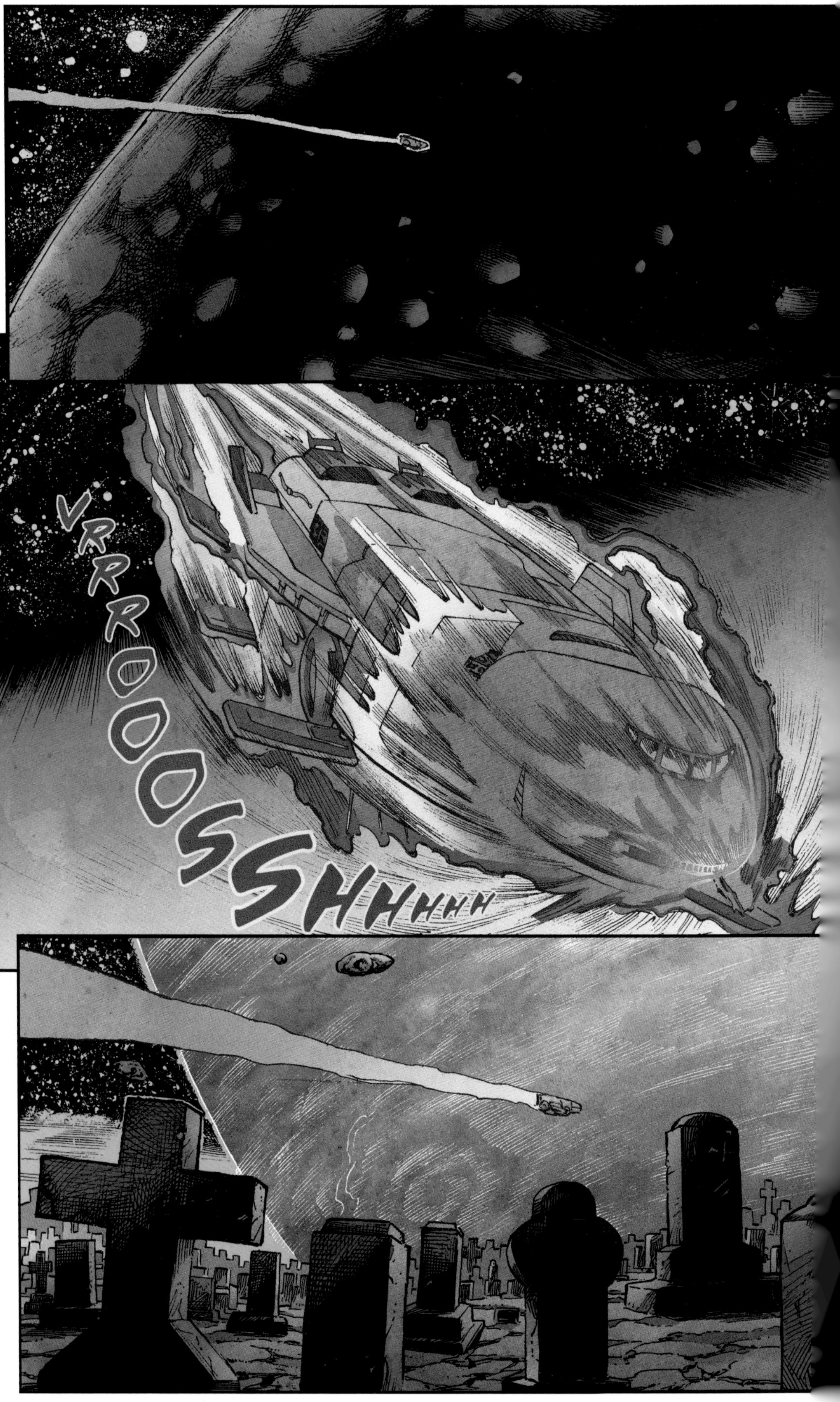
VRRROOOSSHHHHH

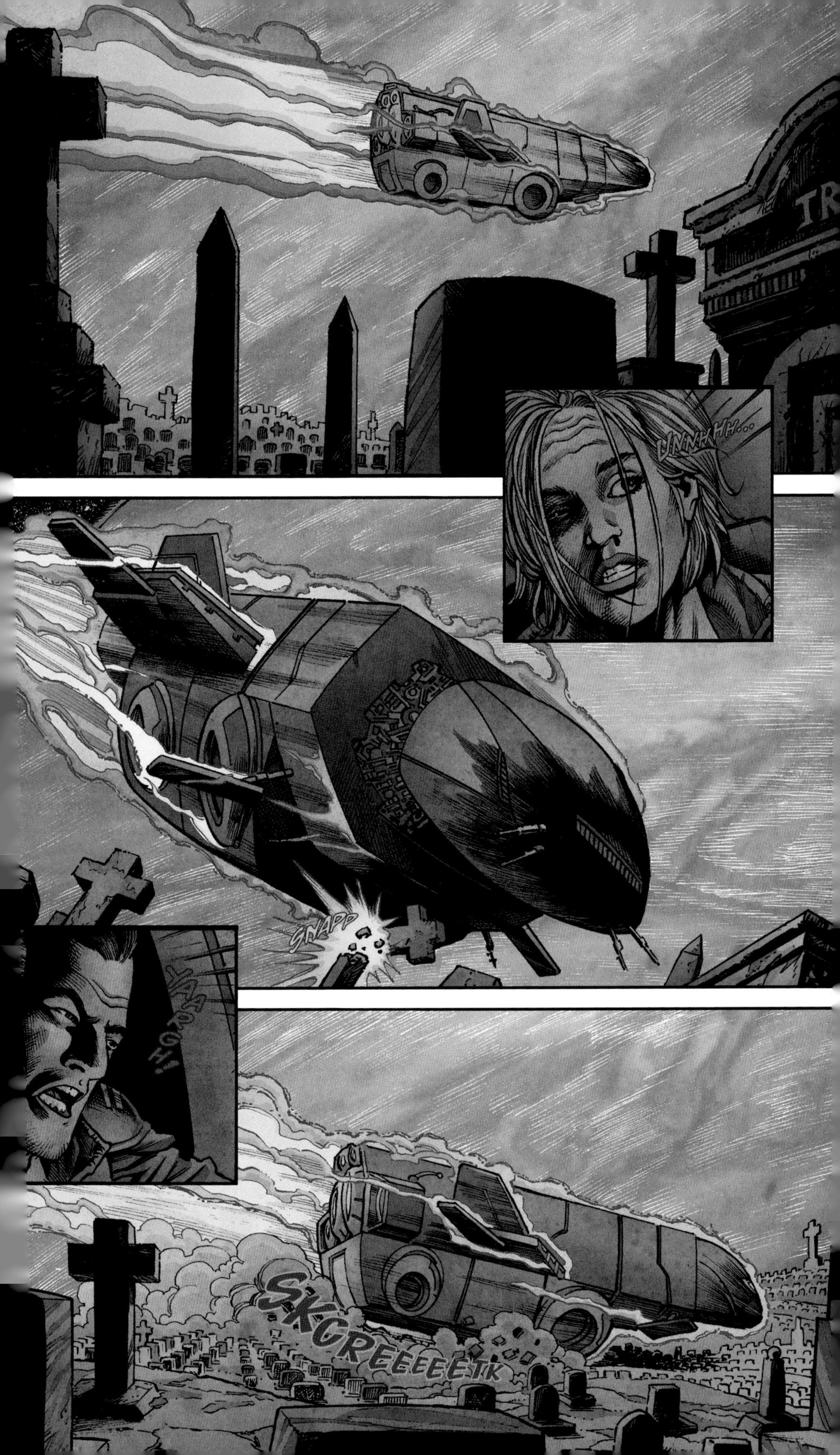
UNNHHH...
GNAPP
YAAGGH!
SKGREEEEEETK

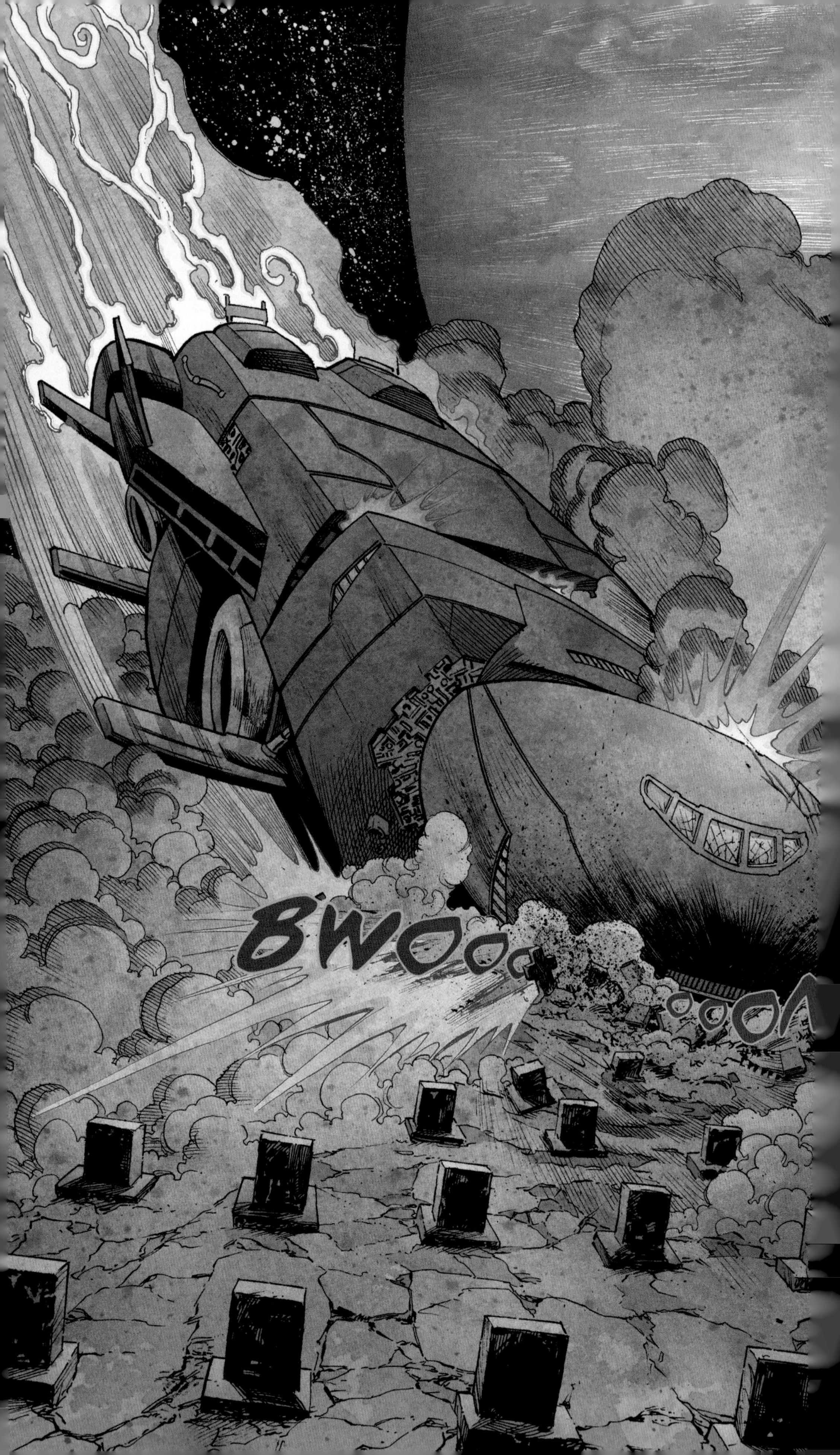
BWOOO
OOOO

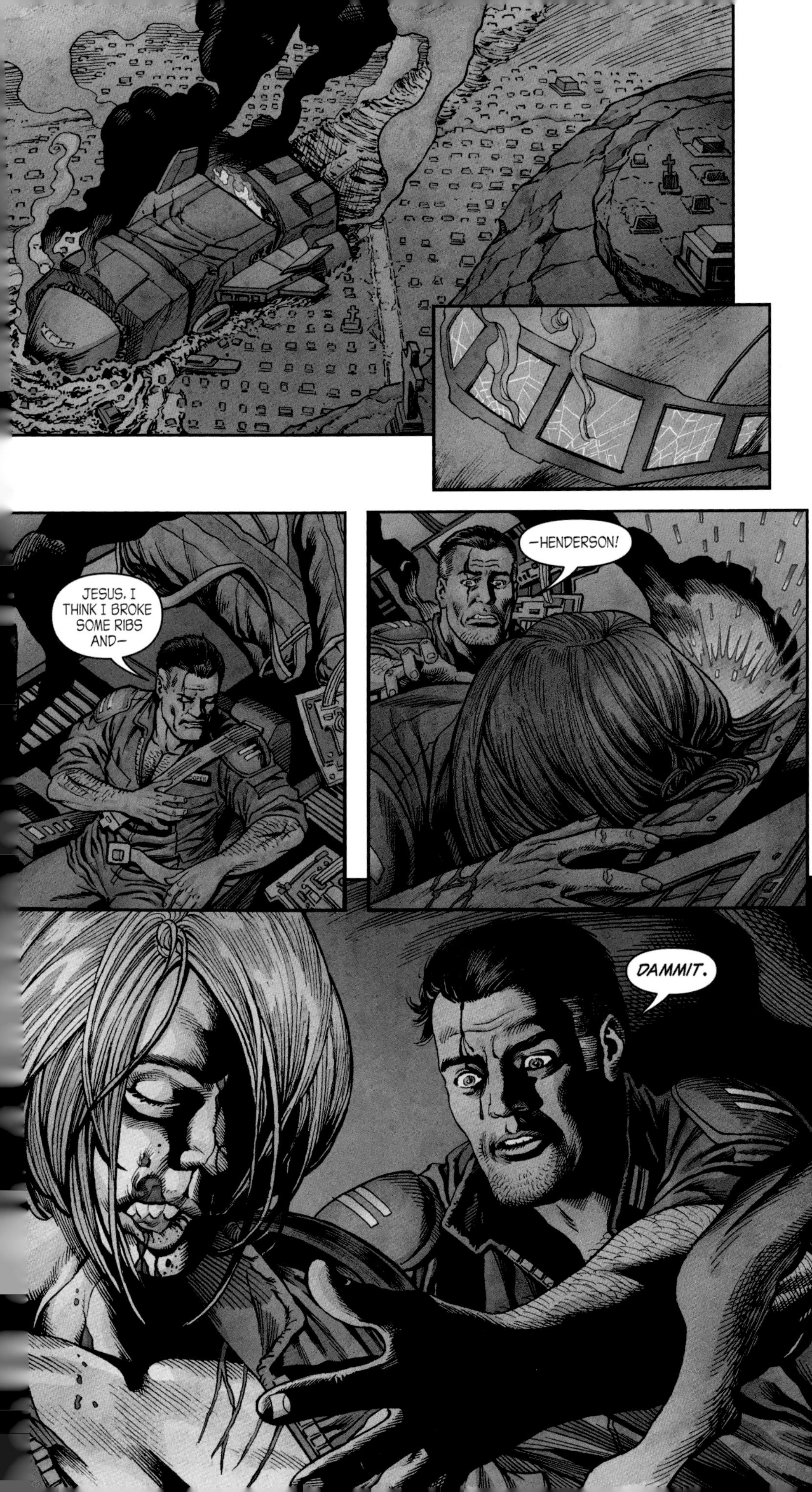
JESUS. I THINK I BROKE SOME RIBS AND—
—HENDERSON!
DAMMIT.

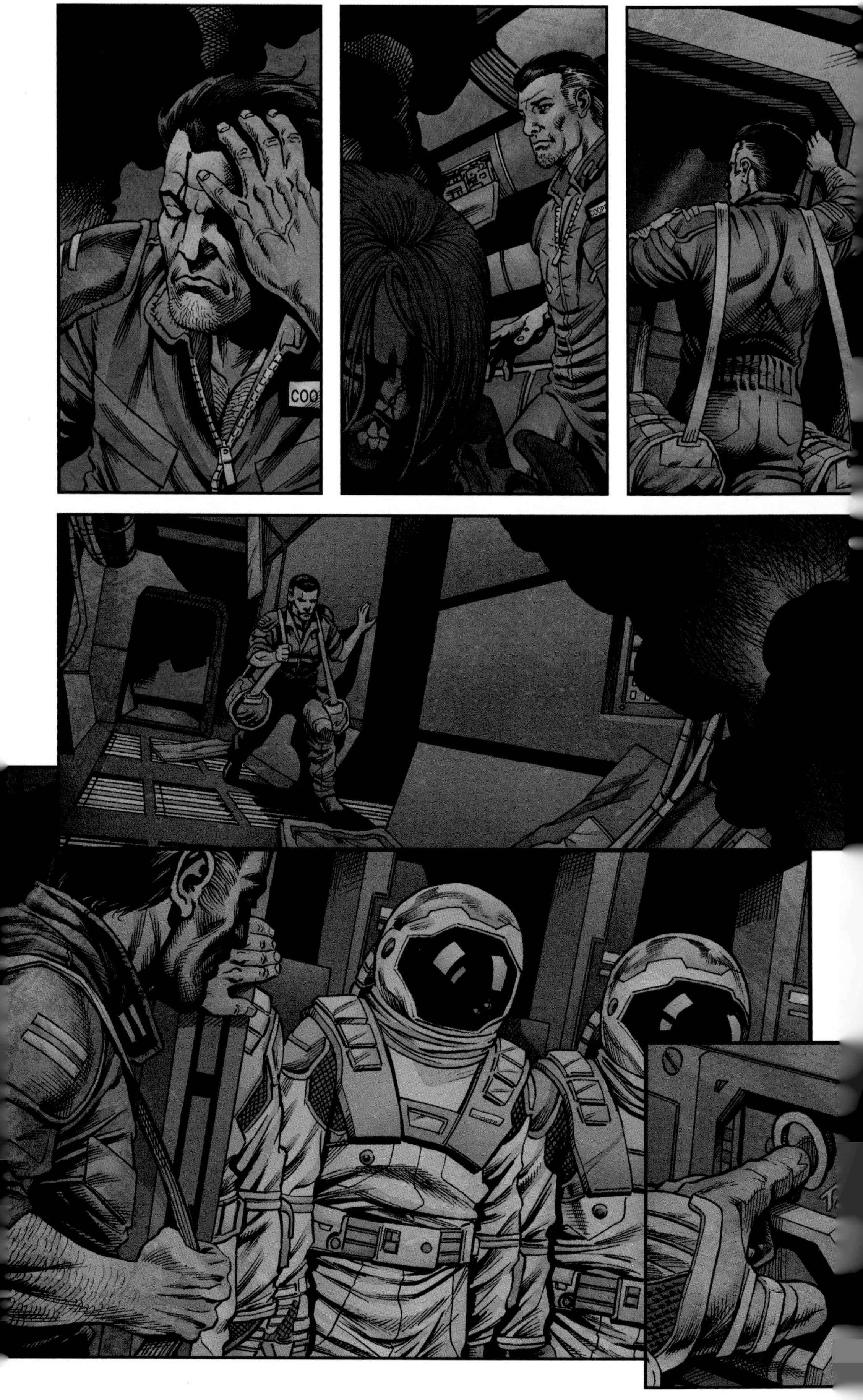
COO
COOP
COOPER

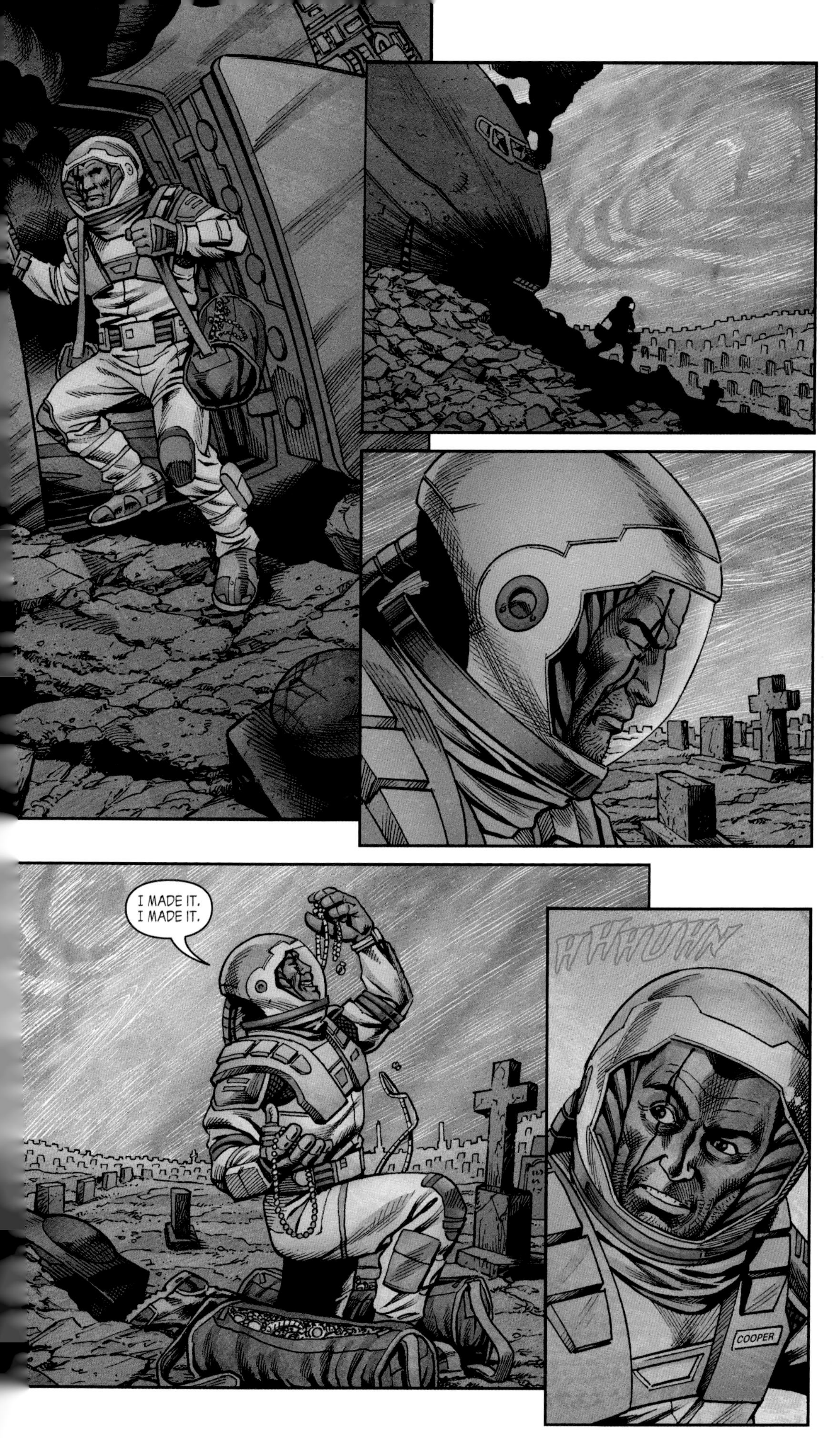
I MADE IT. I MADE IT.
HHHUHN
COOPER

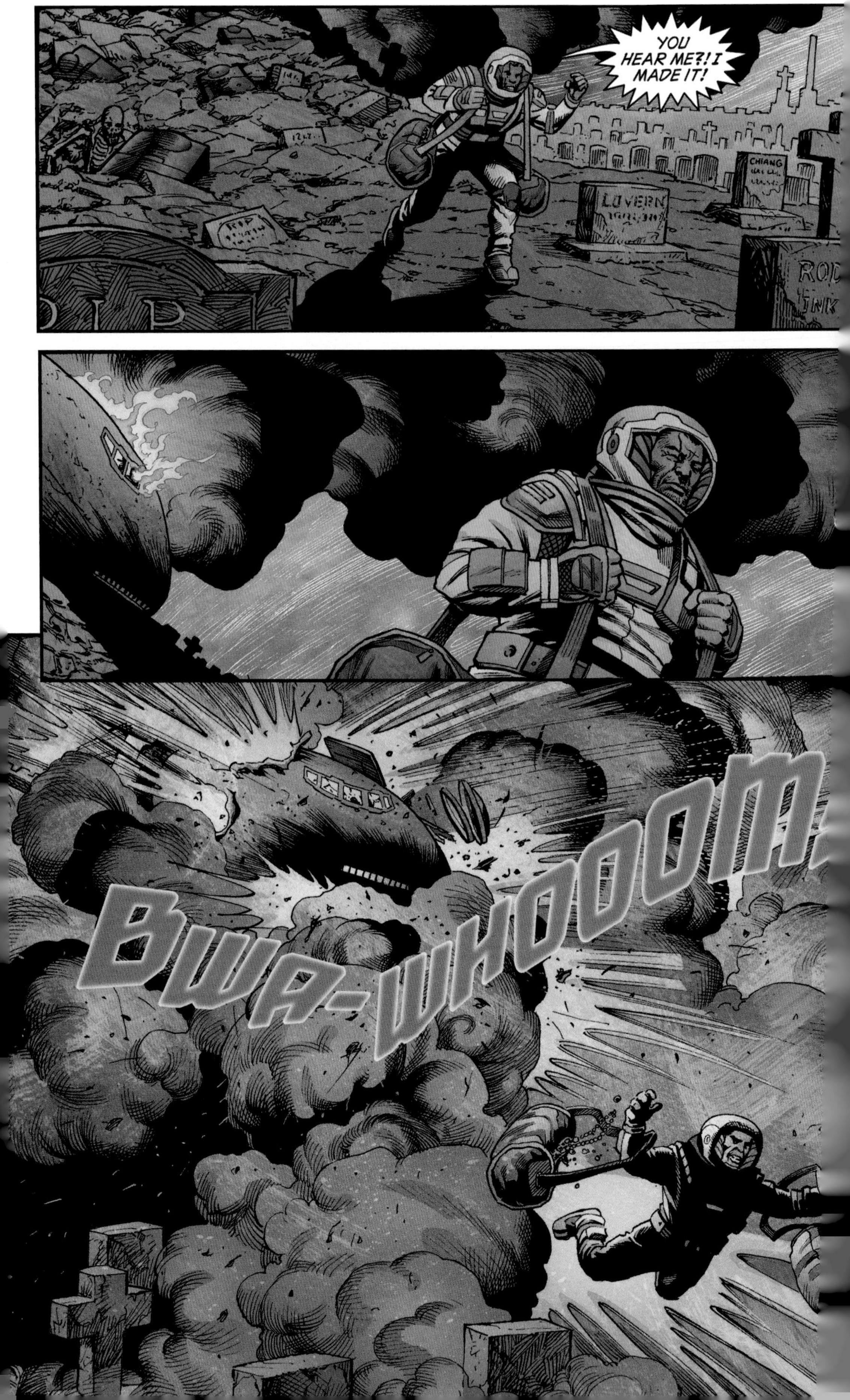
YOU HEAR ME?! I MADE IT!
LOVERN
CHIANG
BWA-WHOOOOM

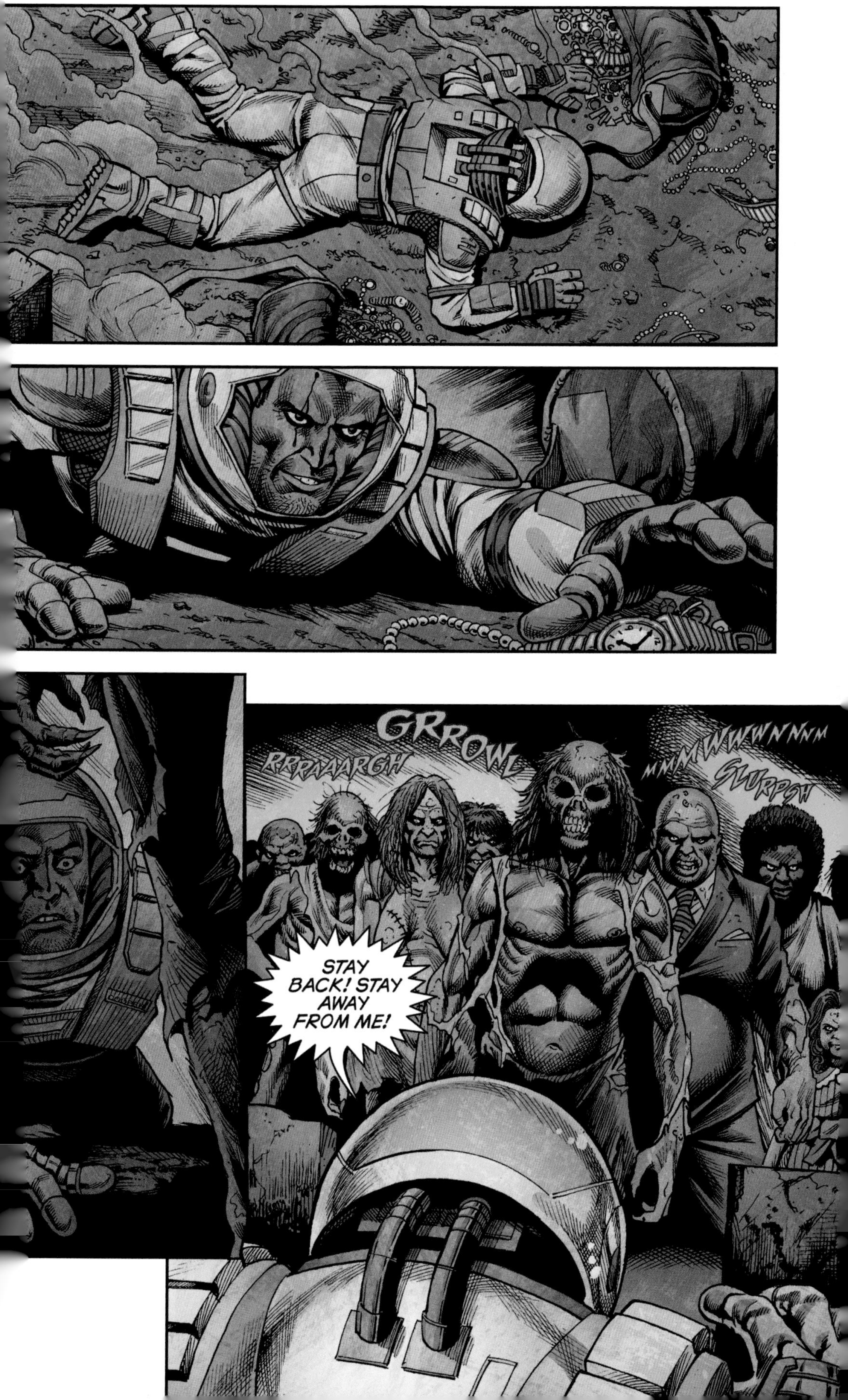
GRROWL
RRRAAARGH
MMMWWWWNNNM
SLURPGH
STAY BACK! STAY AWAY FROM ME!

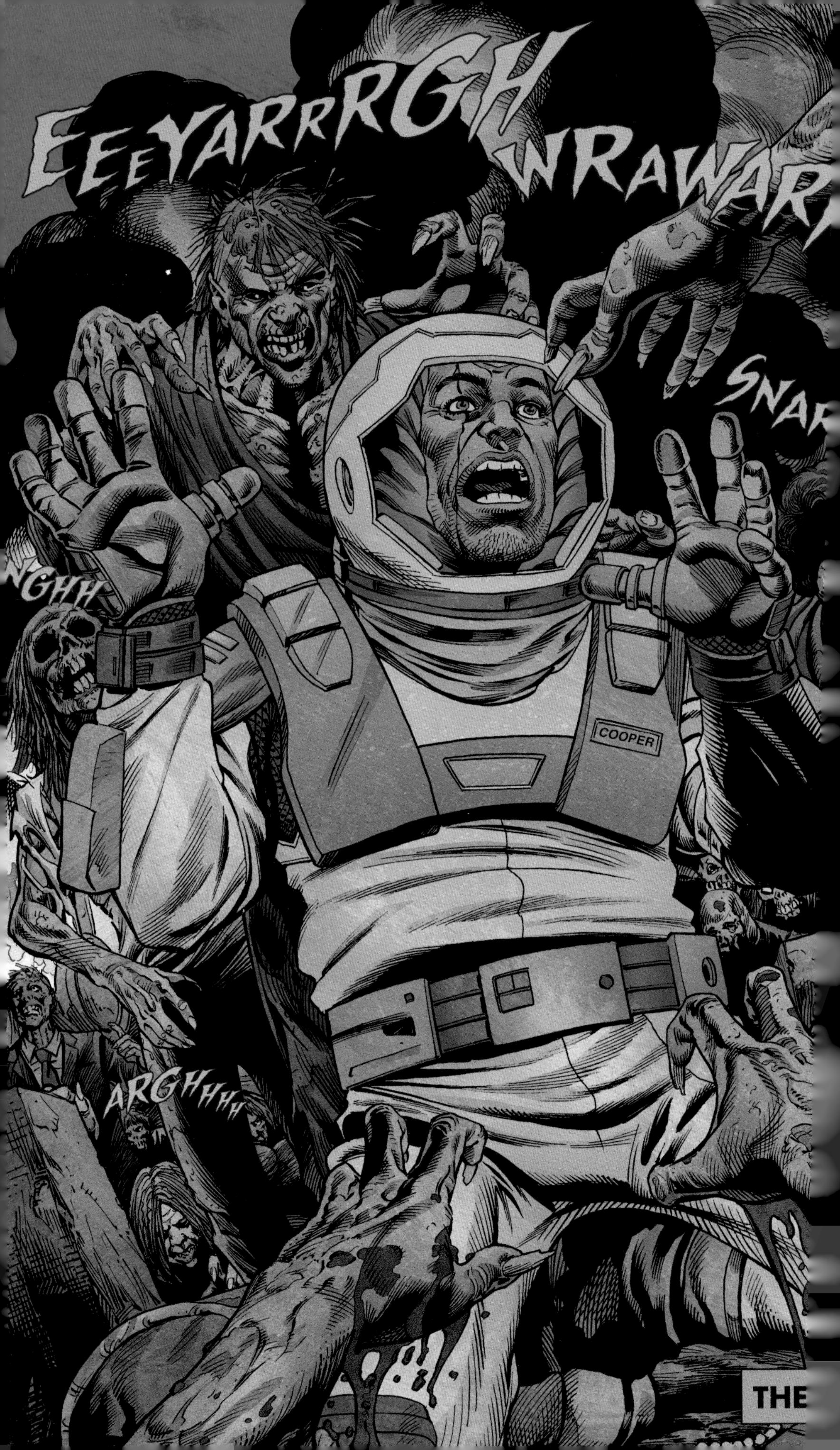
EEEYARRRRGH
WRAWARR
SNAR
NGHH
COOPER
ARGHHHH
THE

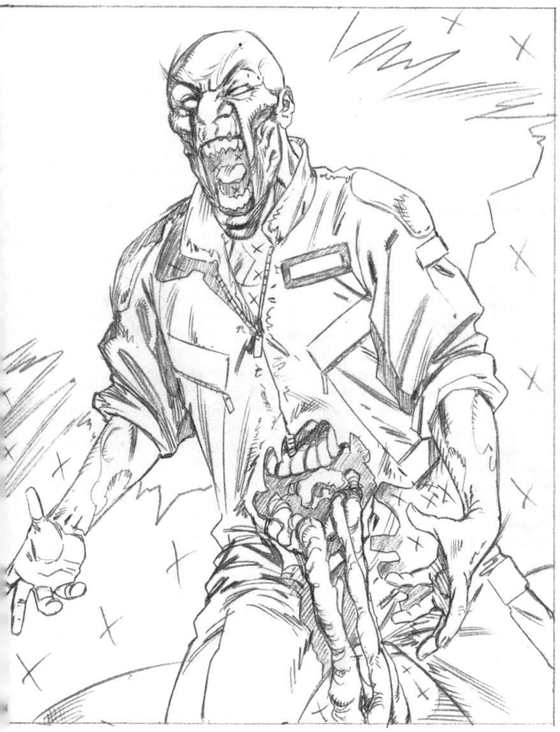

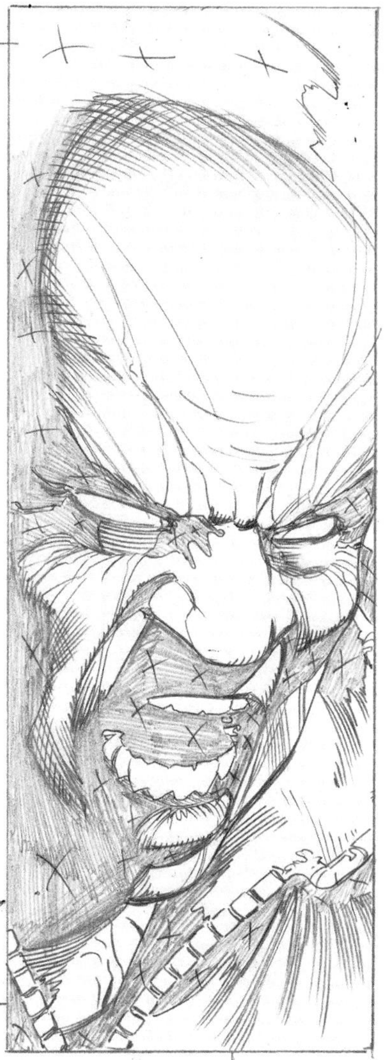

The ART of

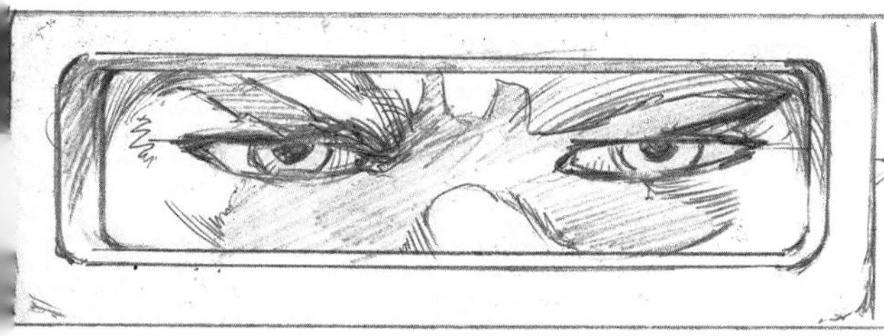

RAVEYARD MOON

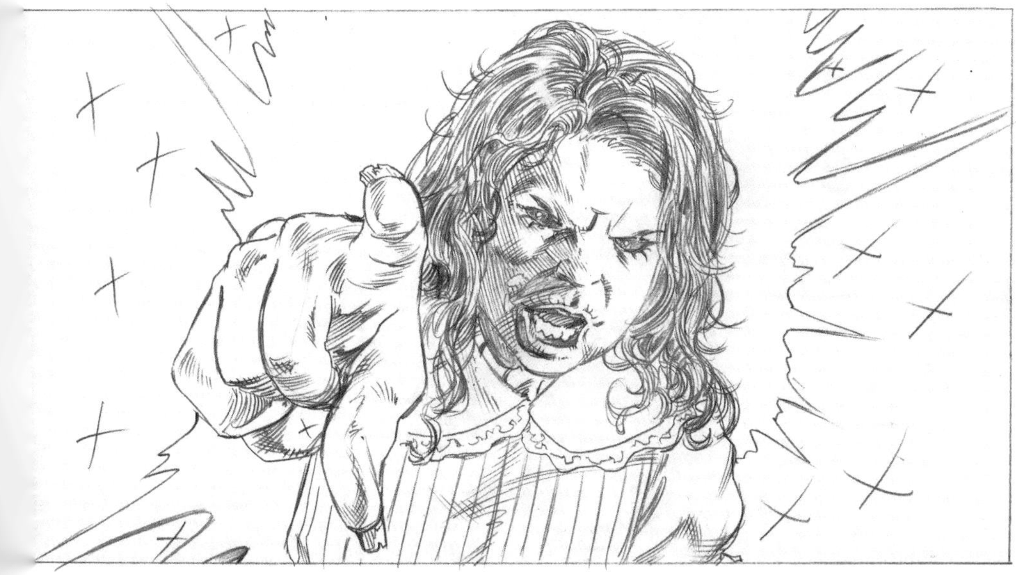

HENDERSON

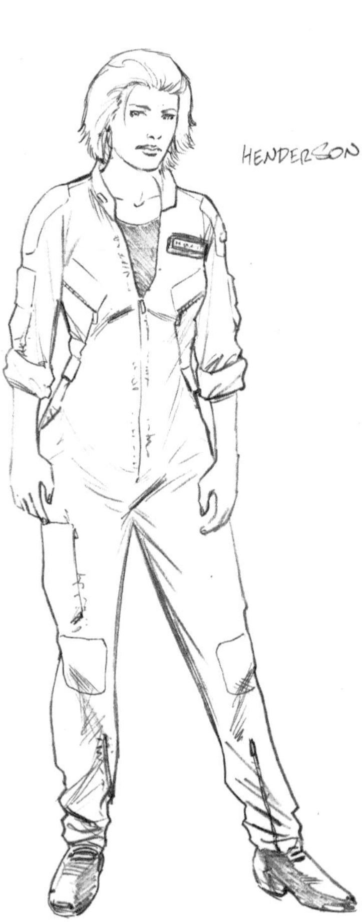

COOPER

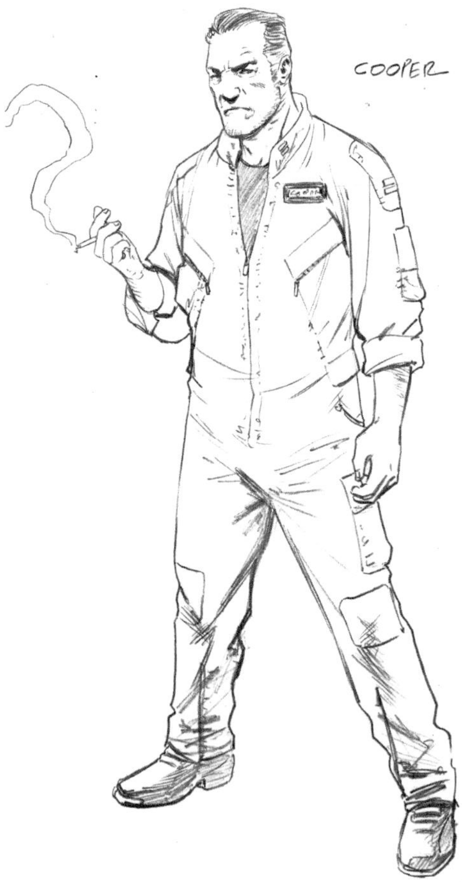

COLE

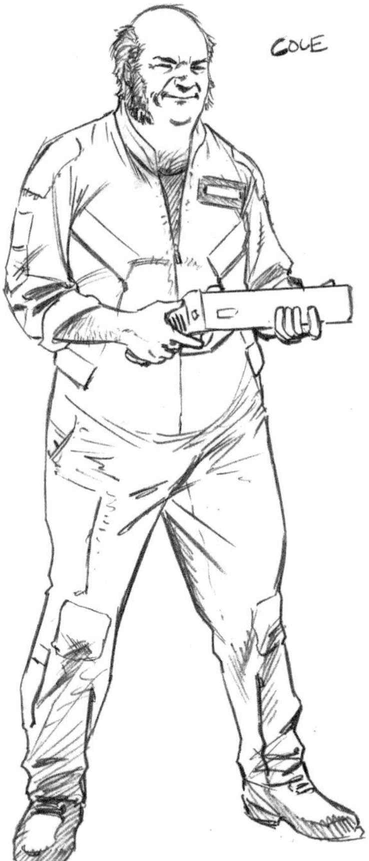

KNOX

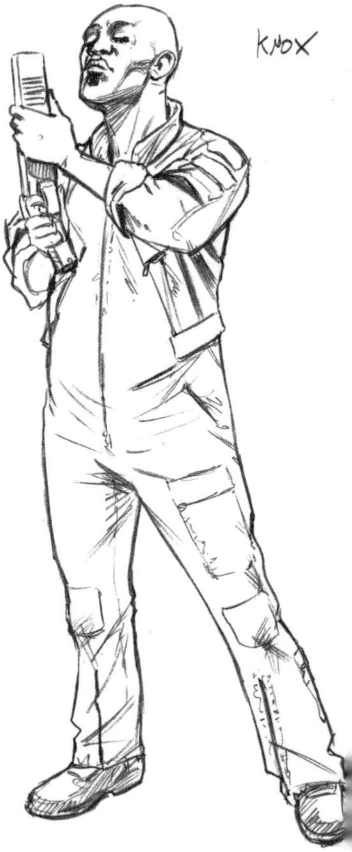

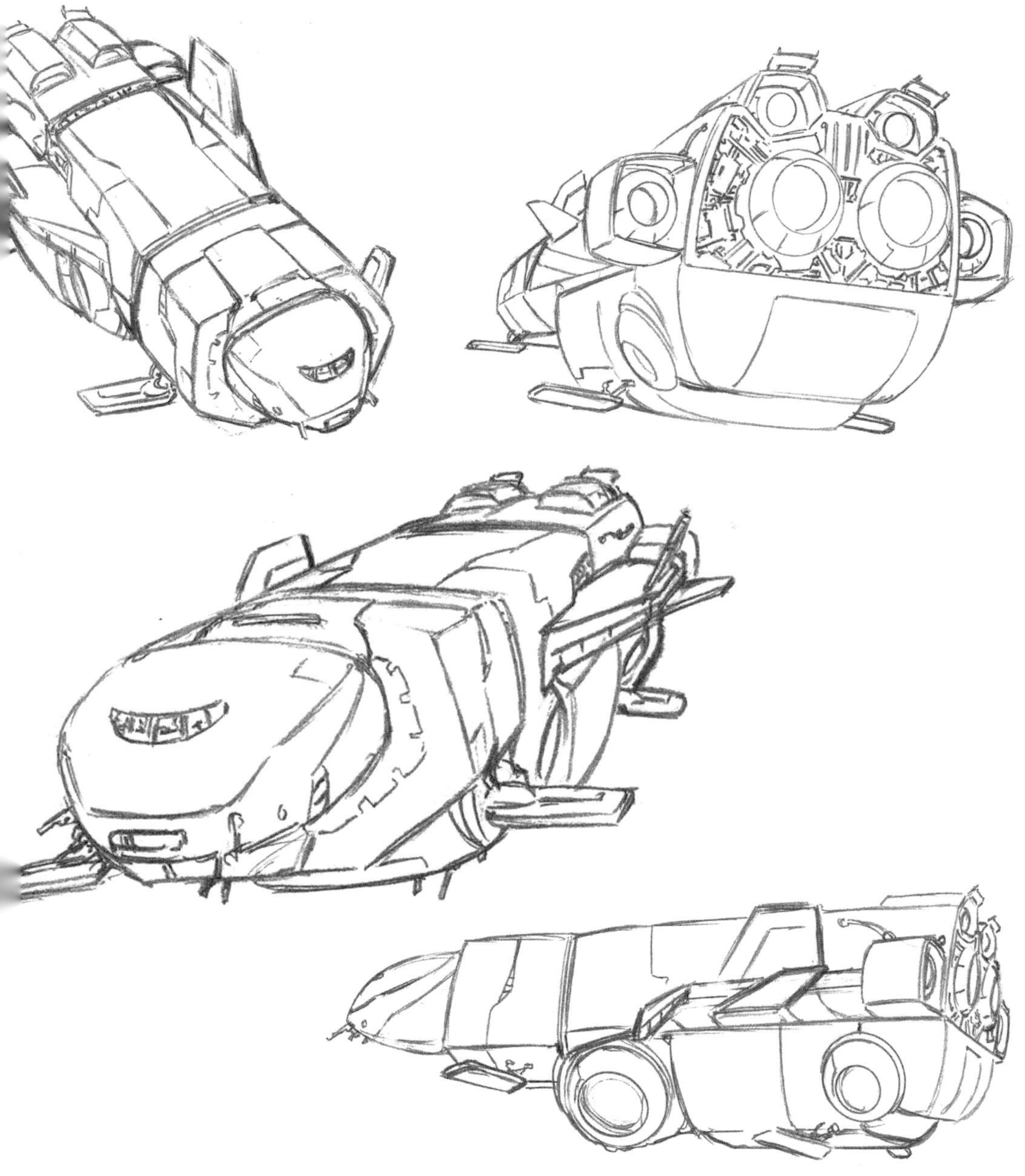

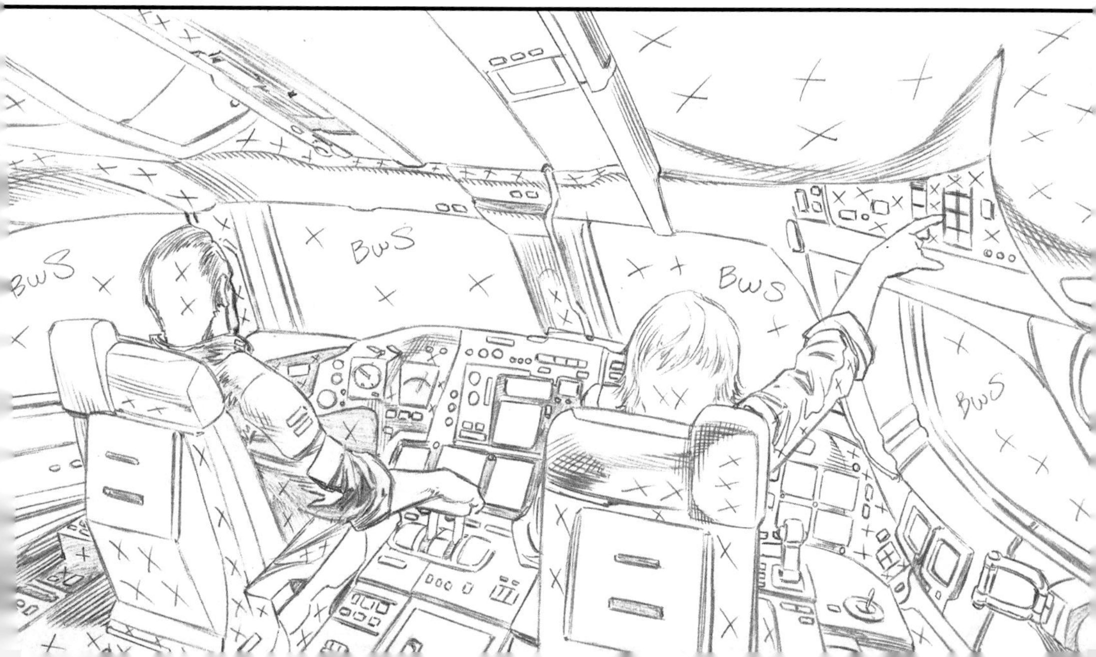
BwS
BwS
BwS
BwS

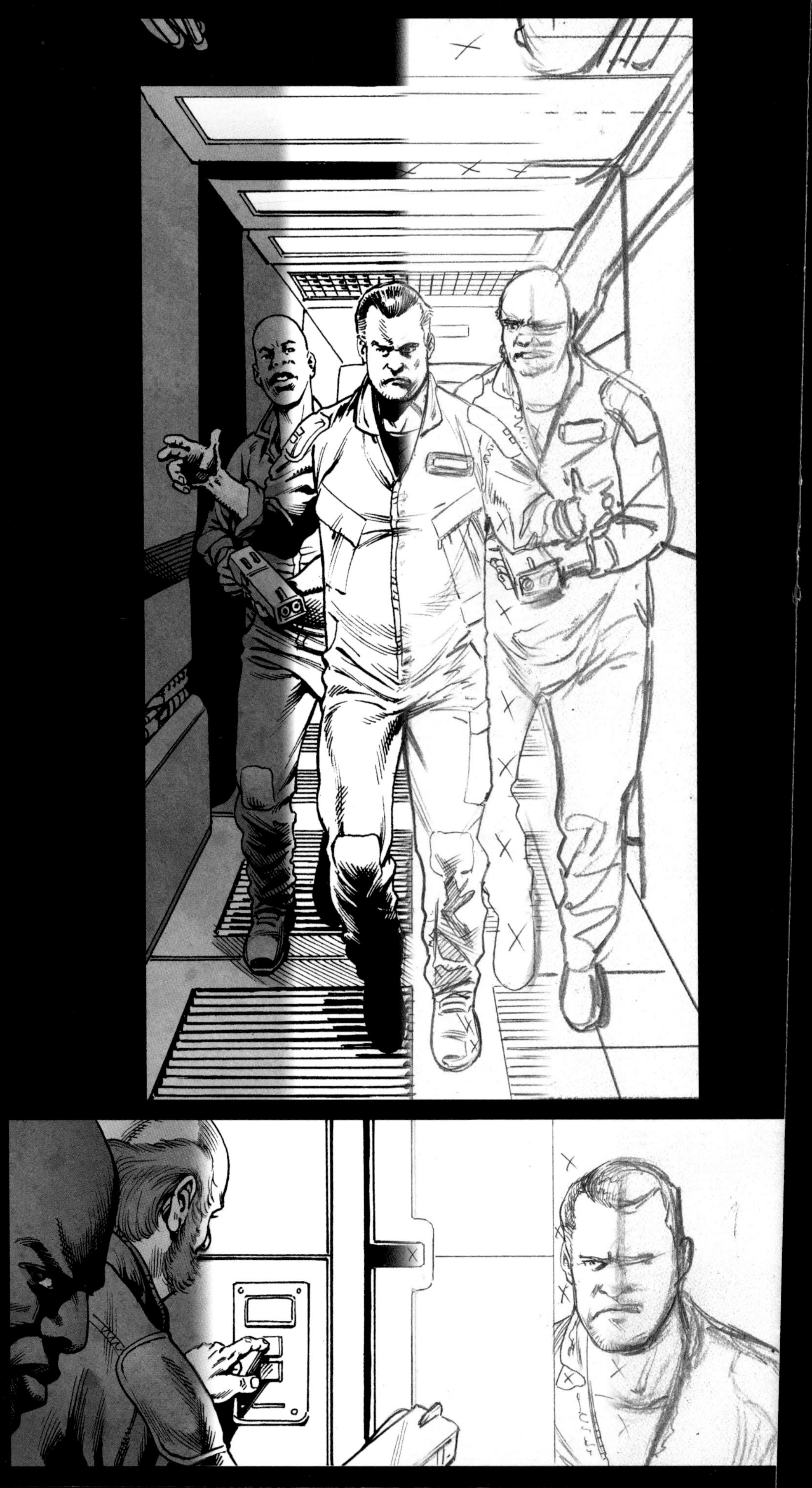

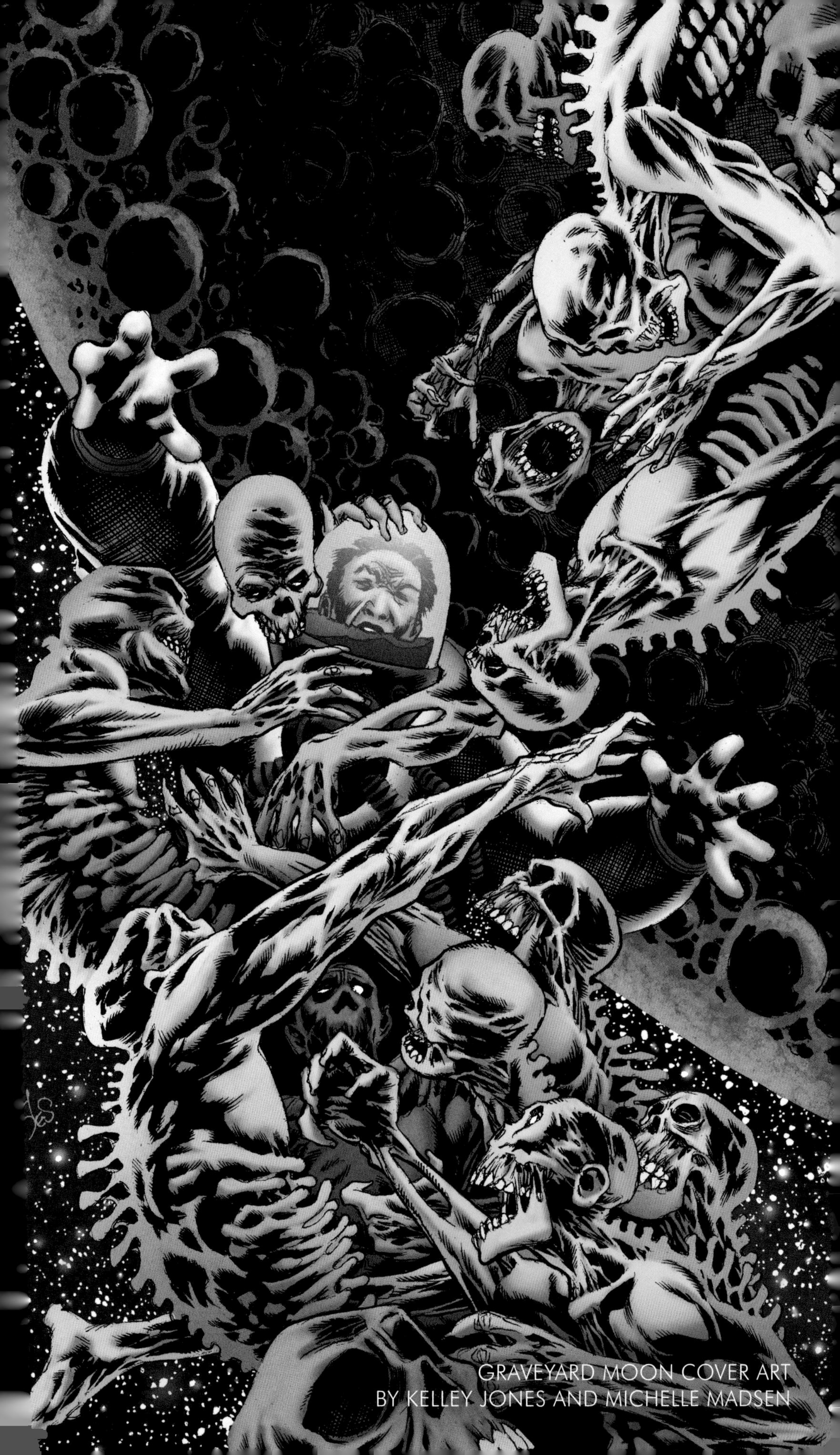

GRAVEYARD MOON COVER ART
BY KELLEY JONES AND MICHELLE MADSEN

CREATOR BIOS

PHOTO BY KYLE CASSIDY

PHOTO BY DAN SANTONI

NO
WHINING

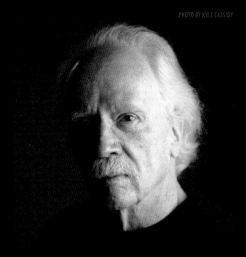

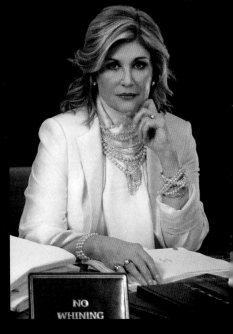

JOHN CARPENTER

John Carpenter's films are legendary: from the breakthrough ***Halloween*** (1978) to classics like ***Escape From New York, The Thing, Big Trouble in Little China*** and ***They Live***. His sci-fi love story, ***Starman***, earned Jeff Bridges a Best Actor Oscar nomination.

For the small screen, Carpenter directed the thriller ***Someone's Watching Me***, the acclaimed biographical mini-series, ***Elvis***, and the Showtime horror trilogy ***John Carpenter Presents Body Bags***. He also directed two episodes of Showtime's ***Masters Of Horror*** series.

He won the Cable Ace Award for writing the HBO movie, ***El Diablo***.

In the gaming world, he co-wrote the video game ***Fear 3*** for Warner Bros. Interactive.

In the world of comics, Carpenter co-wrote the BOOM! books ***Big Trouble in Little China*** with Eric Powell and the ***Old Man Jack*** series with Anthony Burch. He also co-wrote DC's ***Joker: Year Of The Villain*** with Burch. At Storm King Comics he is the co-creator of the award-winning series, ***John Carpenter's Asylum*** and the acclaimed annual anthology collection, ***John Carpenter's Tales for a HalloweeNight***, as well as ***John Carpenter's Tales of Science Fiction***, ***John Carpenter Presents Storm Kids***, and the newest line, ***John Carpenter's Night Terrors***.

SANDY KING

Artist, writer, film and television producer ar CEO of Storm King Productions.

With a background in art, photography ar animation, Sandy King's filmmaking career h included working with John Cassavetes, Franc Ford Coppola, Michael Mann, Walter Hill, Jo Hughs and John Carpenter.

She has produced films ranging from pub service announcements on Hunger Awarene to a documentary on astronaut/teacher Chri McAuliffe, and major theatrical hits like ***Th Live*** and ***John Carpenter's Vampires***. Fr working underwater with sharks in the Baham to converting 55 acres of New Mexican des into the vast red planet of Mars, new challen interest and excite her.

The world of comic books is no exception. It allo her to bring her art and story telling experie to a new discipline with an expanded group collaborators. Through Storm King Com she has created and written the award-winn ***Asylum*** series, the multiple award winn ***Tales for a HalloweeNight*** anthologies, both created and edits the monthly series, ***J Carpenter's Tales of Science Fiction***, ***J Carpenter Presents Storm Kids***, and newest line, ***John Carpenter's Night Terro***

Writer **STEVE NILES** is best known for *30 Days Of Night, Criminal Macabre, Simon Dark, Mystery Society,* and *Frankenstein Alive Alive*.

Niles currently works for comic publishers including Black Mask, IDW, Image and Dark Horse. He wrote *The October Faction* for IDW, which is now a Netflix series.

30 Days Of Night was released in 2007 as a major motion picture. Other comics by Niles, including *Remains, Aleister Arcane* and *Freaks Of The Heartland,* have been optioned for film.

Steve lives in the desert near Los Angeles with his wife Monica and a bunch of animals.

STEPHEN B. SCOTT has illustrated such titles as *Batman, X-Men Forever, JLA, Marvel Adventures Hulk, Indiana Jones and the Tomb of the Gods,* and many more. Over his twenty plus year career, the publishers he's worked with have included DC Comics, Marvel Comics, Image, Dark Horse, I.D.W., and several independent publishers. His most recent work can be found in the Award Winning adaptation of Neil Gaiman's *The Graveyard Book* and the critically acclaimed series *Normandy Gold* from Titan Comics, along with several covers for their Hard Case Crime line.

RODNEY RAMOS has been a professional comic book illustrator for over 30 years. He began his career at Marvel Comics doing art corrections under the direction of the legend John Romita. He started penciling for Marvel on such titles as *Marvel Comics Presents, Psi-Force, What-If, Thundercats* and *Conan*. He then went on to inking a wide variety of books like *Punisher War Journal, Amazing Spider-man,* and *Ironman*. Over the years he has worked for many publishers including Marvel, Marvel U.K., DC Comics, Valiant, Acclaim, Disney Publishing, Titan Comics, Legendary Pictures Comics and Lion Forge. His inks have graced over 500 issues, from *Spider-man* to *Batman* to the critically acclaimed Vertigo series *Transmetropolitan*.

LOVERN KINDZIERSKI has been recognized by the Comic Buyer's Guide survey as one of comics' most influential colorists of all time. He has designed color for every major publisher in the industry and been nominated several times as Best Colorist for both the Eisner and Harvey Awards.

JANICE CHIANG is a comic pioneer as one of the first female lett[er] in the industry. From hand-lettering to digital, she has forged the wa[y] countless female comic artists. Janice works with publishers old (Ma[rvel] and new (DC's Ringo Award winning **Supergirls**). Comics Alli[ance] honored Chiang as Outstanding Letterer of 2016 and ComicBook gave her the 2017 Golden Issue Award for Lettering. In May 2 Chiang was featured as one of 13 women who have been making c[omics] since before the internet on the blog Women Write About Comics. her kind and forthright nature, Janice has built a loyal family withi[n] comic community.

Considered one of the legendary horror comic artists of all time, **KE[LLEY] JONES** came to prominence on DC's **Deadman**, creating a h[orrific] skeletal vision of him. This lead to his classic run of **The Sand[man** **Season of Mists** with Neil Gaiman. Jones then went on to **Ba[tman] & Dracula: Red Rain**, wherein the Caped Crusader beca[me] vampire. Jones became most known for his utterly unique turn [on] **Batman** monthly series with writer Doug Moench, creating a noir masterpiece with the title.

Recently he's brought his delicious and dark work to **Swamp Thin[g** Len Wein and again with Batman and Scarecrow in **Batman: Ki[ng of] Fear**, as well as **Daphne Byrne** for Joe Hill's DC imprint, Hill H[ouse]

MICHELLE MADSEN lives in Portland with her husband an[d] black cats. She has been coloring comics for over 20 years. Rece[nt work] includes **Lady Killer Volume 2, Vinegar Teeth, Daphne** Joe Golem** and **Witchfinder**.